Heirloom Sewing
for Today

Heirloom Sewing
for Today

Classic Materials,
Contemporary Machine Techniques

Sandy Hunter

Sterling Publishing Co., Inc.
New York
A STERLING/LARK BOOK

Author's Acknowledgements

The combined efforts of many people have helped develop the art of "French" sewing by machine. Sarah Howard Stone and Melissa Stone, Margaret Pierce, Martha Pullen, Cindy Foose, Kathy McMakin, Mildred Turner, Florence Roberson, and Elizabeth Travis Johnson are just a few of the pioneers in this craft.

And let the beauty of the Lord our God be upon us; and establish thou the work of our hands upon us; yea, the work of our hands establish thou it.   — *Psalm 90:17*

Editor: Carol Parks
Art Director: Celia Naranjo, Dana Irwin
Photography: Evan Bracken, Light Reflections
Production: Celia Naranjo
Illustrations: Olivier Rollin
Editorial assistance: Valerie Anderson

Library of Congress Cataloging-in-Publication Data
Hunter, Sandy.
      Heirloom sewing for today : classic materials, contemporary
machine techniques / Sandy Hunter.
          p. cm.
      "A Sterling/Lark book."
      Includes index.
      ISBN 0-8069-9556-4
      1. Machine sewing. 2. Fancy work. I. Title.
TT713.H85   1997
646.2'044—dc20   96-44346
                                                         CIP

10 9 8 7 6 5 4 3 2 1

A Sterling/Lark Book

Published in 1997 by Sterling Publishing Co., Inc.
 387 Park Avenue South, New York, NY 10016

Created and produced by Altamont Press, Inc.
 50 College Street, Asheville, NC 28801

© 1997 Sandy Hunter
Patterns pages 124-127 © Sandy Hunter

Distributed in Canada by Sterling Publishing,
   c/o Canadian Manda Group, One Atlantic Ave., Suite 105, Toronto, Ontario M6K 3E7
Distributed in Great Britain and Europe by Cassell PLC,
   Wellington House, 125 Strand, London WC2R 0BB, England
Distributed in Australia by Capricorn Link (Australia) Pty Ltd.
   P.O. Box 6651, Baulkham Hills Business Centre, NSW 2153, Australia

Every effort has been made to ensure that all information in this book is accurate. However, due to differing conditions, tools, and individual skills, the publisher cannot be responsible for any injuries, losses, or other damages that may result from the use of the information in this book.

Printed in Hong Kong
ISBN 0-8069-9556-4

Contents

Introduction

I N TRYING TO RECALL THE POINT at which my interest in sewing began, I asked my mother what she could tell me. She remembered an incident that took place when I was about 4 years old. She came into my room to find me mending a stuffed toy elephant that had been loved too hard. Where the needle came from, and who threaded it for me, neither of us could figure out. Sewing, espe-

cially with heirloom-quality materials and time-honored techniques, has been my means of creative expression ever since.

Not so long ago, when a special garment was created for a wedding or christening or to mark another of life's milestones, it was painstakingly sewn by hand with the finest materials the maker could afford and with the best

workmanship possible. The resulting garment was meant to be handed down for generations, continuing to evoke wonderful memories of the occasion and the people involved. The same care was lavished upon household accessories, items for the trousseau, and special-occasion gifts. The ornate laces and fine fabrics often used for such garments and accessories called for

some specialized sewing techniques, now refered to as "French handsewing."

We are fortunate that with today's sewing machines we can sew the most delicate laces and fabrics with ease, and we can replicate the French handsewing techniques with excellent results and in a fraction of the time. The techniques, all described on the following pages, are not complicated, but they may be unfamiliar to even experienced sewers.

We are also fortunate in having access to a magnificent array of very fine machine-made laces at fairly reasonable prices. We can find linen and cotton fabrics with the beauty and durability essential to heirloom projects.

Heirloom sewing today still implies attention to quality, combining the best available materials with the most careful workmanship to create a garment or item that will continue to express the sentiments of its creator for years to come. You can be satisfied that, when your heirloom piece is given as an elegant gift, the recipient—whether a bride, a baby, or a special friend—will long appreciate the extra care you have taken with planning and preparation.

I. Materials
FOR HEIRLOOM SEWING

The materials traditionally used for heirloom sewing are characterized by quality. Fabrics are the finest available, usually very light and fine. Laces and embroidered trims are delicate and exquisitely made. Garments or home accessories that combine these beautiful materials are delightful to wear and use, destined to be treasured by generations to come.

MATERIALS FOR HEIRLOOM SEWING can often be found in stores that stock quality fabrics. There are mail order sources, too, that specialize in heirloom sewing fabrics and trims. Many of these advertise in magazines featuring sewing and Victoriana.

Estate sales, vintage clothing shops, and even flea markets can provide some pleasant surprises in the form of antique laces. A vintage garment, too tattered to wear, may have a fine lace trim that can be removed and reused.

Laces

For the garments and accessories shown on the following pages, the French Valenciennes, or "Val," and Maline laces are used for many of the pieces. Val laces are fine quality and very delicate, a good choice for embellishing rather sheer fabrics. They may be pure cotton, or may contain a very small percentage of nylon for stability.

Most lace designs are available in white, but some come in ecru and "champagne" shades, too. White laces can be tinted with coffee or tea to darken them.

The right side of a lace can be determined by looking at the heading, or border. On the wrong side, it appears bolder, with small thread ends sometimes visible in the design.

Inexpensive nylon or polyester laces are not for heirloom sewing. They don't have the soft, pliable character of the French laces, and they do not work well with heirloom sewing methods.

CATEGORIES OF LACES

Laces are grouped according to the way they are used, or applied.

Insertion

Both sides of the lace have a straight edge, or heading, enabling it to be sewn between two pieces of fabric or to other laces. Insertions range in width from very narrow to several inches wide. Because the lace is so delicate, it would not maintain its shape if it were too wide. When an area of greater width is needed, it is obtained by joining strips to achieve the desired size.

To gather insertion, or to ease it around a curve, pick out a thread from the heading and draw it up.

Edging

On edging, one edge is finished with a design, such as a scallop pattern. The other edge is a heading like those on insertion, into which are woven heavier threads that can drawn up to shape or gather the edging. Edging is attached along its straight edge to fabric or another lace, with the decorative edge providing the finish to the work. Edging, too, is available in a range of widths.

Galloon

Galloon has two decoratively finished edges. It can also incorporate beading for ribbon. It is strong enough to be used for straps on camisoles and lingerie.

Beading

Beading is characterized by holes, or eyelets, along its length, through which ribbon can be threaded. Beading can be an insertion type, or edging, or galloon. It is available in a range of widths, and in patterns to coordinate with a variety of lace designs. It is both decorative and functional; at a neckline, waist, or cuff, the ribbon threaded through it can be drawn up to gather in fullness.

LACE FAMILIES

French laces are often available as "families," with different widths of edging and insertion—and sometimes beading—all of one design. The lace shown at right in the lower photo is a combination insertion, edging and beading.

Swiss Embroidered Trims

Imported embroidered trims are manufactured with machines that produce trims of superior quality. Swiss embroideries, finely worked on a background of very fine cotton, are the best choice for heirloom sewing projects. The background fabric is usually white, and the embroidered design may be white or colored. Many of the Swiss embroideries feature eyelet patterns. Because the design is on fabric rather than mesh, embroideries are stronger than the French laces. Like the laces, embroideries are divided into categories according to the ways they are used.

Entredeux

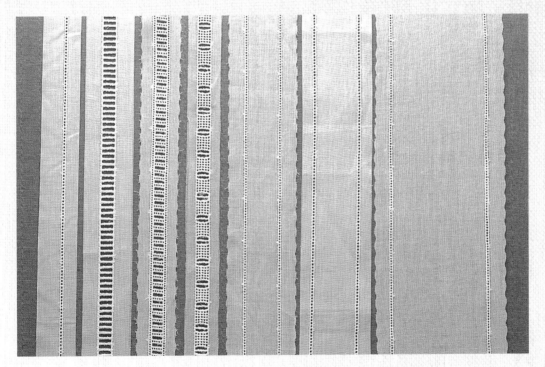

A French word meaning "between two," entredeux is used both as a functional material and as a decorative one. It is sewn between strips of lace or embroidery, or between trim and fabric, to strengthen the seam. Used this way, it also plays an important part in the design of an heirloom piece.

Like the other trims, entredeux comes in a variety of widths. "Wide track" entredeux, such as the three pieces at right in the photo, has a fabric strip between rows of holes to accommodate hand or machine embroidery. Entredeux sometimes has very wide openings, like the piece second from left, and can function as a beading. Other types of embroidery—insertion, beading or edging—sometimes incorporate entredeux on one or both edges. This saves a step when attaching the embroidery to fabric or to another trim.

Embroidered Insertion

As with lace, embroidered insertion is meant to be sewn between other trims or fabrics. It is available in different widths and in a great array of designs that often can be intermixed very successfully. The piece at right in the photo has entredeux along both sides of the design area.

Embroidered Edging

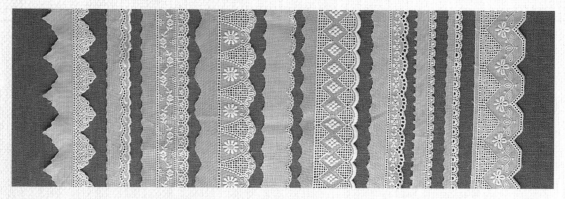

Entredeux is sometimes incorporated, as shown in some of the examples in the photo. Embroidered galloon also is available in some designs, with both edges finished decoratively.

EMBROIDERY FAMILIES

Embroidered trims, like laces, can be purchased as families. The same design often is available on beading, and on insertion and edging in a range of widths.

Many of the newer computerized sewing machines are capable of producing beautiful embroidered designs on lightweight fabrics. Experimentation can be enjoyable, and the results can be magnificent.

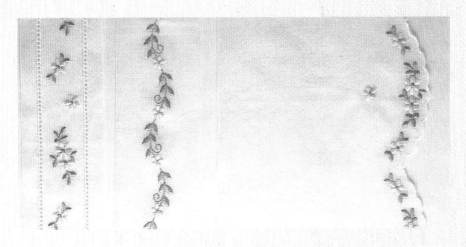

Embroidered in delicate pastel colors, the same design is shown on insertion in two widths and edging. One insertion incorporates entredeux along both edges.

Combining Laces and Embroideries

Mixing patterns and types of trim with exquisite fabrics is one of the creative aspects of heirloom sewing. The possibilities are virtually unlimited! Embroidered trims with different designs can work very well together as long as the background fabrics are similar in color and texture. Two or more lace patterns can add interest to a design, too, if their mesh backgrounds are compatible.

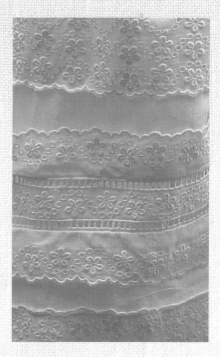

embroidered or lace "fabric" is stronger than its delicate appearance suggests, and can comprise an entire yoke or collar.

Joining the different types of lace and Swiss embroidery calls for some special sewing techniques. Detailed instructions begin on page 20.

Creating Fabric With Lace and Embroidery

Many of the projects in this book begin with the construction of a block of laces or embroideries. Strips of lace, or embroidery, are joined one to another to create a single larger piece. The resulting

Fabrics for Heirlooms

Natural fiber fabrics—cotton, linen, silk, and wool—are the best choice for heirloom sewing. Fabrics suitable for their compatibility with the laces and embroideries are very light in weight and of very fine quality, most imported from Switzerland or France.

For heirloom sewing, the most suitable fabrics are lightweight, fairly soft materials made from natural fibers. Left to right: "albatross" wool challis, Viyella, cotton organdy, silk organdy, silk batiste.

The specialized sewing techniques called for in heirloom sewing work far better with natural fiber fabrics, especially cotton and linen, than on synthetics or blends. Pintucks and rolled and whipped edges are much easier to achieve, and seams can be sewn and pressed smooth and flat. If ease of care is a requirement for your project, or if you are devoted to blends and abhor ironing, search out the best quality polyester/cotton batiste.

Batiste
The most popular fabric for heirloom sewing and one that is easy to sew is cotton batiste. It is woven of very fine threads and is available in several very light weights. The best quality cotton batiste is from Switzerland, translucent fabrics with beautiful surface luster. Silk batiste, with the characteristic silken sheen, is an elegant fabric for heirloom sewing. It is a superb choice for special-occasion projects.

Lawn
Cotton lawn is somewhat heavier in weight than batiste, but still very delicate. It is an easy fabric to sew and press, a natural for heirloom techniques. Lawn fabrics are often found printed with small floral patterns.

Voile
Cotton voile has a slightly more open weave than lawn or batiste and is made with slightly heavier threads. It is very light and airy, with a hint of crispness.

Dotted Swiss
Fine cotton fabric, such as lawn, has an overall pattern of miniscule dots that can be woven into the fabric or flocked onto it.

Organdy
The crispness of cotton organdy is a result of the fabric's construction rather than finishing agents, so is retained through laundering. Silk

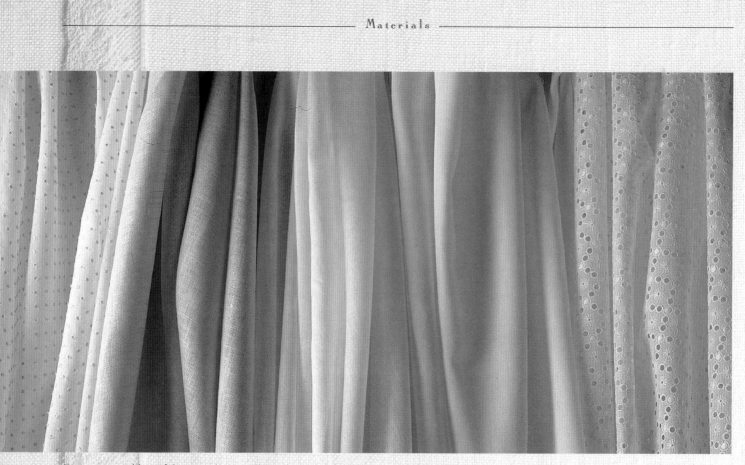

Fine cotton and linen fabrics work especially well with heirloom sewing techniques. Left to right: Swiss cotton with all-over embroidered dot pattern, handkerchief linen, lightweight Swiss cotton batiste, medium-weight cotton batiste, cotton eyelet.

organdy, a luxurious alternative, has the same crisp hand as well as the surface sheen associated with silk.

Linen

Handkerchief weight and other lightweight linen fabrics are excellent for heirloom sewing techniques and projects. Despite its delicate appearance, linen is a strong fiber that washes and wears well. It is sometimes blended with cotton or ramie to produce a less costly fabric that is also easy to sew.

Silk

Lightweight, plain weave silk fabrics such as batiste and broadcloth can be fine choices for some heirloom projects. Silk requires a bit more care than cotton does, but these silk fabrics are no more difficult to sew, nor are they necessarily more expensive, than cotton of comparable quality.

Wool

Very lightweight wool is another good fabric choice that is not always associated with heirloom sewing. Very fine quality wool flannel or challis, for example, is perfectly compatible with French laces and adapts well to heirloom sewing techniques. Challis that is a blend of wool and cotton has beautiful draping qualities, washes and wears well, and can be less expensive than pure wool.

Non-traditional Fabrics

Some of the projects in this book combine traditional heirloom materials with fabrics that are not usually associated with heirloom sewing—wool tweed and heavy linen, for example. Contrasting weights and textures can be mixed successfully with striking results. Try French lace with raw silk, or perhaps Swiss embroidered trim on corduroy. Experimentation, after all, is half the fun of sewing.

Accents and Notions

Findings and embellishments for heirloom projects should be of the same good quality as the fabric and laces you choose. Small details can make a big difference in the appearance of the finished work.

Thread

For the delicate materials usually used in heirloom sewing, lingerie weight thread is the best choice. Stitches will be nearly invisible on lace, and seams will not be too thick for the materials they are connecting. The manufacturers of quality threads all offer the fine weight thread, either in all cotton or cotton-wrapped polyester.

Closures

Mother-of-pearl buttons, not plastic, are the traditional choice for heirloom garments. They are available at quality fabric stores and from mail order sources, and can often be found at flea markets and antique shops.

If your closure design requires a row of closely spaced buttons, as they often are placed down the back of a wedding or christening gown, for example, look for the time-saving "bridal loops." Elastic loops are sewn along a strip that can be inserted in a seam or placket.

Some projects call for snaps instead

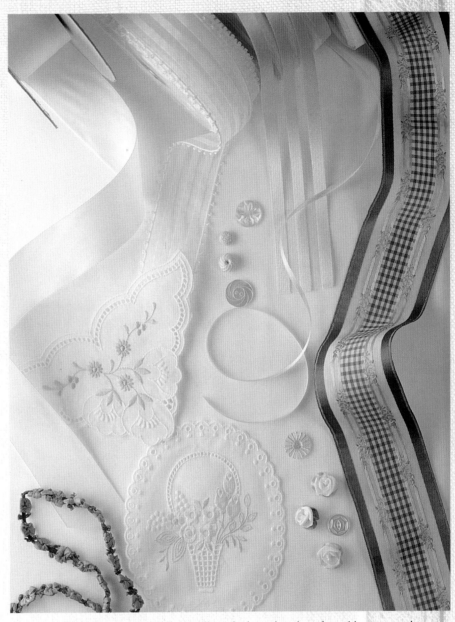

French ribbons, embroidered medallions, silk rosebuds, and mother-of-pearl buttons can be used creatively to accent heirloom pieces.

of buttons. Best are small, nearly invisible clear ones. Remember to keep the hot iron away from them.

Small, decorative pins, called "beauty pins," are another heirloom sewing tradition. The most popular of these are gold pins and enameled pins with floral designs. A beauty pin may be just the thing when a single fastener is needed at the neckline, for example. And they are a great boon to the sewer who dislikes working buttonholes.

Ribbon

When ribbon is part of a design, look for the very best quality to enhance the appearance of your work. A good choice is double-faced polyester satin ribbon, available in a range of widths, colors, and novelty designs. A quality ribbon will be soft and pliable.

Silk ribbon adds a touch of luxury. It may be difficult to locate, but worth the trouble for a special project. For a really elegant effect, try embroidered French ribbon like that used for the ring bearer's pillow pictured on page 114.

To draw in fullness at the waistline of a garment or around the lower edge of a sleeve, a ribbon woven through beading is preferred over the use of elastic in heirloom garments. Elastic usually will wear out far sooner than the fine materials used in heirloom garments.

Decorative Accents

Heirloom materials suppliers may stock a variety of beautiful, ready-made embellishments that can be used to accent your piece or that can be the focal point of a design. Details like silk ribbon roses or an embroidered medallion require a good bit of time to make; it is handy to know you can purchase them in finished form.

Bias Bindings

Sleeve and neckline plackets and armhole finishes often call for bias binding. Commercial double fold bias tape is usually made of synthetic blend fabric that is too heavy for use with heirloom materials. It is quick and easy to make custom bias bindings from your garment fabric. The complete instructions begin on page 40.

Tools and Equipment

Heirloom sewing does not require any special gadgets or tools that aren't found in a reasonably well equipped sewing room. There are a few tools and notions, though, that are especially helpful for working with the fragile laces and light-weight fabrics.

YOUR SEWING MACHINE

Most machines with zigzag stitch capability can be used for heirloom sewing. With fine materials, it is especially important that the feed mechanism and tension are adjusted correctly. It is also important to keep the machine cleaned and oiled according to the machine manufacturer's instructions.

Needles

For sewing fine fabrics and laces, it is essential to use a fine needle that is in good condition. For most of these materials, a 65/9 or 70/10 needle will work best. Change the needle frequently, and always change it if it strikes a pin during sewing. A damaged point can cause pulled threads or poor stitch quality on fine fabrics.

Presser Feet

For most machines, there are many presser feet available that are designed for specialized sewing techniques. For heirloom sewing, an edge stitch foot is particularly helpful. Your dealer can tell you of others that may be useful.

The Serger

For overcasting seams, a serger is a great time-saver. As with the sewing machine, it is especially important when sewing fine materials to be sure the needle sizes are compatible with the materials and that the points are undamaged. Check that the lower knife blade is free of nicks. Keep the serger free of lint, and oil it regularly, following the manufacturer's instructions.

Take time to adjust the tension settings. Unbalanced tension is more likely to cause problems with light-weight fabrics than with heavier materials.

Pressing Equipment

A good steam iron is as important to heirloom sewing as to any sewing project. A pressing ham is useful for pressing curved areas, and a sleeve board handy for small areas. The very specialized puffing iron was designed just for this kind of sewing. With it, you can easily achieve a good press in gathered areas such as strips of puffing.

Scissors and Shears

Good, sharp dressmaker's shears will cut fine fabrics cleanly. Appliqué scissors are very helpful for trimming. The extension on the lower blade helps prevent unplanned cuts. For clipping thread ends and trimming in tight places, small embroidery scissors are handy, too.

Pins

For delicate fabrics and laces, long, slender "silk" pins are essential. Glass heads are an added advantage—they make it easier to find and remove pins that are hidden among gathers, and they won't melt if touched by a hot iron. Pins that have dull points should be discarded to prevent damage to fabrics.

Rotary Cutter and Mat

These tools can save hours of time in cutting bias fabric strips for bindings or piping. Used with a see-through ruler, fabric can be cut quickly and accurately.

Bias Tape Makers

Available in several sizes, these handy gadgets enable you to quickly make bias binding from your chosen fabric. The tape maker folds in the edges of a bias strip as you press—and it helps prevent scorched fingers at the same time.

Bodkin

A bodkin is much more efficient than a safety pin for drawing ribbon through beading or a casing. It's less likely to fray the ribbon, too.

Tracing Paper

Heirloom sewing often calls for the addition of new design lines to a pattern: adding a yoke, an inset, or tucks, for example. It is better to trace a copy of the pattern piece for cutting and experimentation than to try to reassemble the original later.

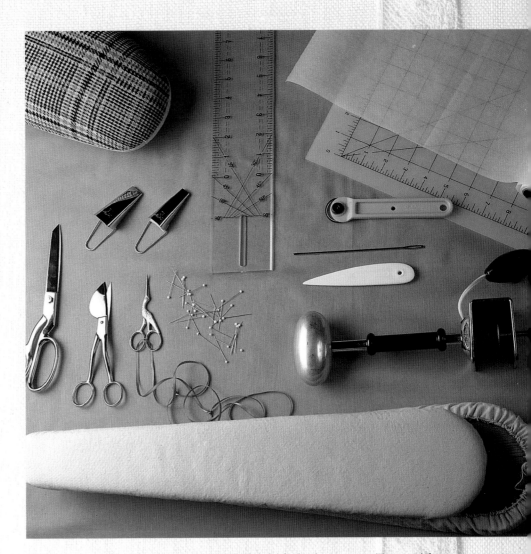

Certain sewing and pressing aids are especially helpful for heirloom sewing. Top row, left to right: pressing ham, see-through ruler, cutting mat, tracing paper. Second row: bias tape makers, rotary cutter, bodkin, point turner. Third row: dressmaker's shears, applique scissors, embroidery scissors, glass-headed pins, puffing iron. Bottom row: sleeve board.

2. Special Techniques
FOR HEIRLOOM SEWING

Heirloom sewing—the creation of garments and home accessories with combinations of fine laces, eyelet trims, tucks, ribbons, and hand sewn embellishments—is a handwork tradition. With the improved precision and increased capabilities of the newer sewing machines, it is possible to replicate the hand sewing techniques in a fraction of the time.

AN ABSOLUTELY ELEGANT HEIRLOOM piece can be constructed entirely by machine. Just a touch of hand needlework, however, can make your work personal and unique. Refer to books on hand embroidery and smocking to find stitches and designs suitable for delicate heirloom garments.

There is nothing difficult about the construction of an heirloom piece, but some of the techniques may be unfamiliar to you if you have never tried this kind of sewing. Even if you are a skilled sewer, take a moment to look through the instructions and tips before you begin.

An heirloom, by definition, is meant to be passed along for generations. Choose the best quality materials and add your best workmanship, and the results will show your care.

Preparing the Materials

If you intend to wash the finished garment or accessory, the components should be washed beforehand to preshrink them and to remove finishing agents. With natural fiber fabrics, it is a good idea always to purchase a little extra fabric to allow for shrinkage. Even if little shrinkage is expected, different materials can shrink by different amounts, giving the piece a

puckered look after it's washed.

Delicate fabrics should be washed by hand, or wash them by machine, at the delicate setting, in a mesh lingerie laundry bag. Use a mild powdered or liquid detergent and lukewarm water. Rinse in cold water to discourage wrinkles.

Smooth out materials and lay them flat to dry. Some can be dried in the dryer at a low temperature setting. Press while damp with the iron on the steam setting appropriate for the fabric. Press with the lengthwise grain of the fabric, taking care not to stretch it. Keep the ironed fabric wrinkle free by rolling it around a cardboard tube or laying it over a clothes rack until you are ready to sew.

For fabrics that will be dry cleaned, steam press them before cutting to preshrink them. If you expect considerable shrinkage with a dry cleanable fabric, ask the cleaner to steam shrink it before you cut.

French laces need not be prewashed, but should be pre-shrunk by pressing them with a steam iron at the cotton setting. The use of a little spray starch can help prevent stretching and make the laces easier to handle when you sew.

Embroidered trims are worked on a cotton ground fabric, so it is a good idea to wash them before sewing. Follow the same procedure

as for other delicate fabrics. If you have yards and yards to deal with, wrap the trim around a plastic or styrofoam piece that will fit into the sink and wash them by hand.

Unwind the trim while it is still damp, and press it right side down on a soft pressing cloth that has a smooth finish. Press with steam, the iron on the cotton setting.

Most ribbon can be swished through lukewarm sudsy water, or can simply be steam pressed. Press with the iron at a low heat setting. Silk ribbon, especially if it is embroidered, may require dry cleaning. Follow the manufacturer's instructions.

DYING LACES

While some laces are available in ecru and champagne shades, the design you like may come only in white. It is easy to tint laces to give them an antique look. Test your "dye" with a scrap of the lace to get an idea of the color and the length of time it will take to achieve the shade you want.

Prepare a cup of strong, hot coffee. Instant coffee can be used, but be sure all the granules are dissolved before adding the lace. Stir in a tablespoon of white vinegar to set the dye. Wet the lace thoroughly and submerge it in the coffee. Check the color after a few seconds: Remove the lace and rinse under cold running water to remove excess color. Repeat the process until the shade pleases you. Different materials absorb color at different rates. Check frequently to avoid getting the color too dark.

Rinse the lace thoroughly in cold water to remove all excess coffee, which could stain the ironing board cover or other materials. Towel blot it, then iron it on a soft cloth with the iron at a cotton setting.

Tea also can be used to dye lace. It usually will produce an apricot tint.

Caring for Heirlooms

An heirloom piece represents quite an investment in good materials and your precious time. It deserves the best of care.

A washable garment or accessory with a great deal of lace, lots of ribbons, or more than a little handwork probably should be washed by hand. Slightly less delicate pieces can be secured in a mesh laundry bag and washed by machine on the gentle lingerie cycle. Use mild detergent or soap, and select a cold rinse cycle.

Remove from the washer as soon as the cycle is finished to prevent setting creases. Roll hand washed pieces in a thick towel to remove

excess moisture. Lay out the piece on a terry towel. Gently re-shape the laces and smooth away creases in the fabric. You will be surprised how much easier it will be to iron the garment! It's when fabric is left wadded up in the washer or dryer that the wrinkles set in.

A piece made of natural fiber fabric—cotton or silk—should be ironed while slightly damp, using steam as well. If you can't iron it right away, use grandmother's trick of wrapping it in a damp towel or plastic bag and storing it in the refrigerator until there is time to iron. A puffing iron is very helpful for difficult-to-reach places.

Getting Ready to Sew

Oil your machine, if necessary, and clean it thoroughly. Install a new, fine needle. Thread the machine with lightweight thread to match the lace or trim.

Press as you sew. When lace is joined to fabric, press seams toward the fabric so they will be less likely to show through. Press embroidered trims from the wrong side, with a soft pressing cloth underneath to prevent flattening the embroidery.

Test stitch length and width settings with a scrap of your fabric.

Fabric Techniques

Trim away the fabric selvages before you begin. Straighten each crossgrain edge of the fabric, if necessary, by pulling a thread to mark the grainline precisely. Snip into the edge of the fabric and gently pull a thread from the cut to create a line. If the thread breaks, lift a new thread from that point along the cut and continue. Cut carefully along the marked line.

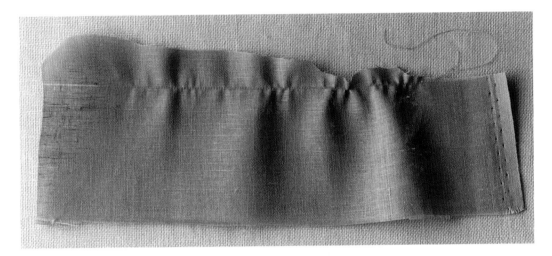

A pulled thread also can be used to mark for straight vertical cuts and to mark foldlines for tucks.

If the edges of your piece will all be finished with lace or trim, the fabric edges can be overcast first with a serger. Use the three-thread overlock for less bulk, and use fine thread.

Roll and Whip

This technique can be used in place of machine overcasting or serging to finish a fabric raw edge before lace is attached. The name of the technique derives from the way it is done by hand: The raw edge is rolled between two fingers to encase the edge in a roll, then a whipstitch taken around the roll to secure it.

To roll and whip by machine, set the machine for a zigzag stitch. Stitch length and width will be determined to some extent by the thickness of the fabric being used. For lightweight cotton batiste, the length might be set at 1.2 mm (approximately 15 stitches per inch) and the width at 3.7 mm.

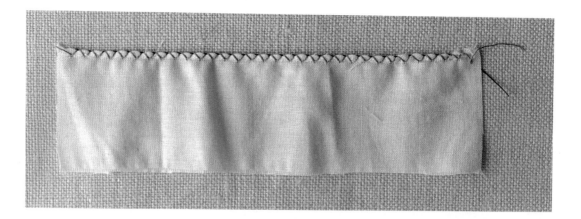

Experiment to find the settings that give the best results with your own machine, thread, and fabric.

Place the fabric right side up. Adjust so that on the right swing the needle goes *just* off the edge of the fabric. The stitching will roll the raw edge and strengthen it. This technique works only with light to medium-light fabrics.

Roll, Whip, and Gather
Method 1
Pull out top and bobbin threads so they are slightly longer than the fabric edge to be gathered. Hold the thread ends in place along the raw edge and roll and whip over it, being careful not to catch the long threads in the stitching. Then just draw up the encased threads to gather the fabric.

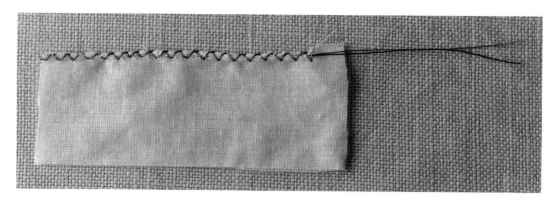

Method 2
Cut a piece of strong thread slightly longer than the piece to be gathered. Anchor it with a good knot at the beginning end of the fabric edge you will gather. Lay the thread along the edge and roll and whip over it, keeping the long thread free of the stitches. Pull the thread end to gather the piece.

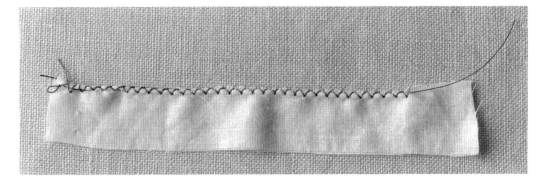

Puffing
This term is used to describe a strip of fabric that is gathered along both edges. The effect is similar to shirring, soft and puffy. Puffing is typically used in skirts, collars, and pillows.

For puffing, begin with a fabric strip twice the desired length of the finished piece. Roll, whip, and gather first one side, then the other.

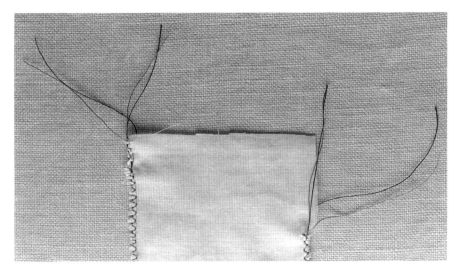

Adjust and align the gathers so both sides of the piece are the same length and the gathers are perpendicular to the edges.

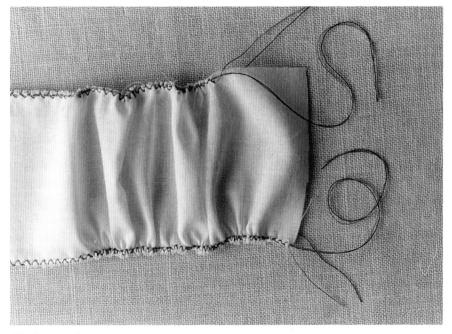

Gathering Fabric

On the fabric right side, stitch two rows of machine basting ¼ and ⅜ inch (.7 and 1 cm) from the raw edge. Pull bobbin threads to gather to desired measurement.

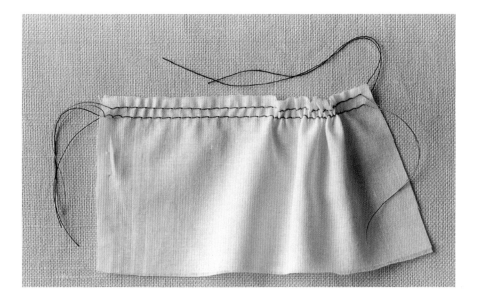

Sewing Laces and Embroidered Trims

The right side of the lace is smoother; the wrong side is rougher, with tiny visible thread ends.

Stitch laces just at the inner edge of the heading, or border. If you stitch within the heading, the needle is likely to strike one of the stronger threads woven into the heading and cause the lace to pucker.

When joining two or more strips of lace, align the patterns across the rows.

When you begin to sew two strips together, leave a tail of each extending behind the presser foot so that you can hold the laces, along with the bobbin and needle threads, as you sew the first few stitches.

Sewing Lace Edging to Fabric
Method 1

With a sewing machine or serger, overcast the raw edge of the fabric before attaching lace. Then place the lace and fabric with right sides together, the lace heading aligned with inner edge of the overcast stitching or the needle stitch of the overlock. Stitch with a straight stitch at the inner edge of the lace heading. Turn right side out, press the seam toward the fabric. Topstitch close to the seamline on the fabric.

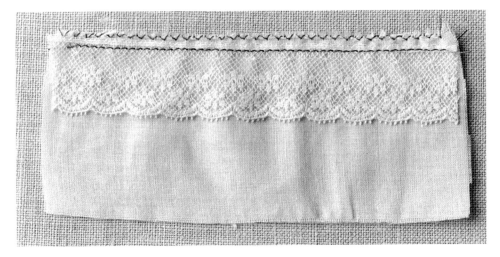

Method 2

Place lace and fabric right sides together, with the edge of the lace about ⅛ inch (3 mm) in from the fabric edge. Stitch with a fairly close zigzag stitch, wide enough that the needle swings just over the lace heading and just over the edge of the fabric.

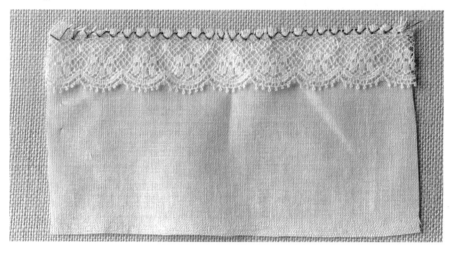

Sewing Embroidered Edging to Fabric

The unfinished upper edge of embroidered edging is often scalloped, and must be trimmed off straight along the low points of the scallops. Edging can be sewn directly to the edge of a piece of fabric with right sides together, using a narrow seam allowance and then overcasting the raw edges. It looks better, however, to use entredeux between the pieces. Follow the instructions for joining entredeux to fabric, pages 30–31.

Sewing Lace Insertion to Lace Insertion

Method 1

Place strips of lace right side up, abutting the edges and lining up the pattern

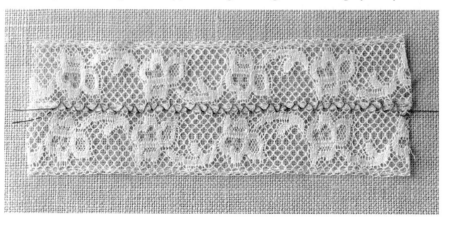

motifs. Sew with a fairly close zigzag stitch, wide enough that the needle swings over both headings, but not into the open mesh of the lace.

Method 2
Place both strips of lace right side up, their headings overlapping. Zigzag them together as above, but with a narrower stitch width.

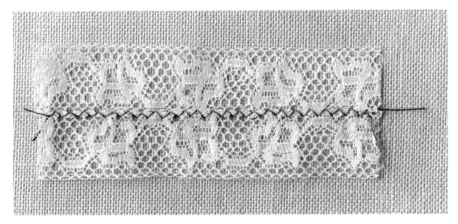

Working with Entredeux

Strips of entredeux are usually placed between rows of laces to add stability, especially when many strips of lace are joined to create a large piece of lace "fabric," as for the yoke of a nightgown. Entredeux also serves as a design element, between laces, or between two pieces of fabric as in the blouse shown on page 73.

Entredeux is in effect a row of holes, with fabric on either side that can be used as seam allowance. In some cases it will be trimmed away, one side at a time, so that you work only with the row of holes.

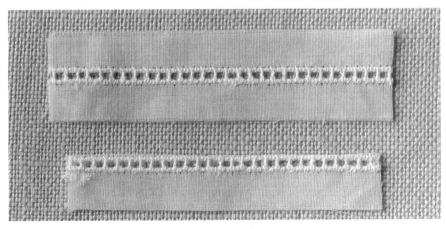

The right side of entredeux is slightly raised, and smooth. The wrong side is flat, and rougher.

When sewing entredeux, set the zigzag stitch length and width so that the needle goes into the center of a hole with each stitch. Practice stitching with an unthreaded machine to find the correct stitch length setting, then thread up and practice on scraps.

Sewing Entredeux to an Unfinished Fabric Edge
Place untrimmed entredeux and fabric with right sides together, aligning raw edges. With a straight stitch, sew right along the row of holes.

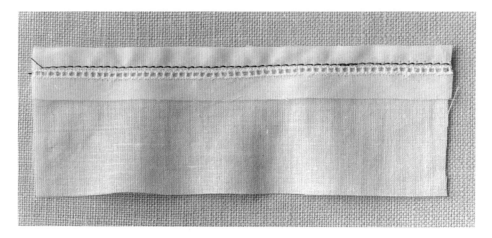

Clean finish the seam allowances. Press toward the fabric.

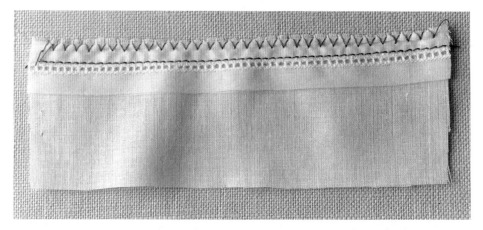

If desired, topstitch close to the seamline on the right side.

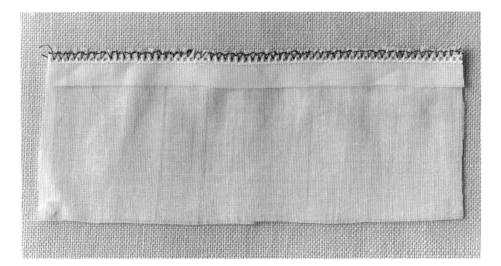

To sew entredeux to fabric with a serger, use a narrow overcast stitch. Place the entredeux and fabric with right sides together and stitch along the border of the holes. Press the seam allowance toward the fabric and topstitch as above.

Sewing Entredeux to a Rolled and Whipped Fabric Edge

Trim seam allowance from one side of the entredeux. With right sides together, place the trimmed edge along the rolled and whipped fabric edge, up against the roll. Sew with a zigzag stitch set so that the needle goes into each hole and just over the fabric edge.

Joining Lace to Entredeux

Method 1

Place the lace, right side up, over the seam allowance of the entredeux—also right side up. Straight stitch along the inner edge of the lace heading. Stitch again with a zigzag stitch set so that the needle goes into each hole of the entredeux and just over the previous stitching line. Carefully trim away the excess entredeux seam allowance from the back.

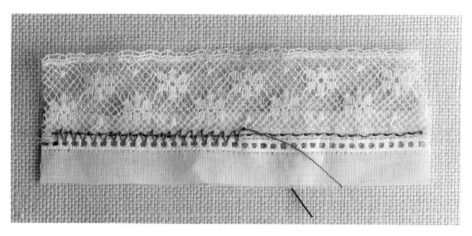

Method 2

Trim one seam allowance from the entredeux and lay it right side up. Place the lace, right side up, with the heading against the trimmed edge of the entredeux. Zigzag over the lace heading and into each hole of the entredeux.

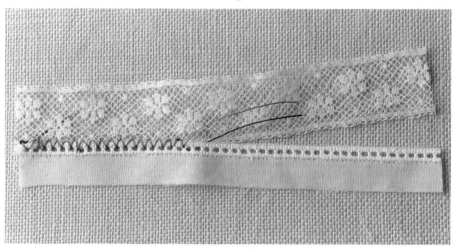

Joining Embroidered Edging to Entredeux

The procedure is the same as method 1 for sewing entredeux to an unfinished fabric edge: Stitch the entredeux and edging with right sides together using a straight stitch and stitching just next to the row of holes. Overcast or serge the seam allowances and press toward the edging.

Sewing Lace Insertion to Lace Beading or Edging
Place a strip of insertion and a strip of beading, or edging, right side up with edges abutted. Stitch with a close zigzag stitch wide enough that the stitch extends across to the inner edge of both lace borders.

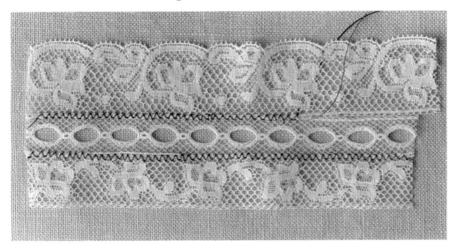

Sewing Fabric with Entredeux to Joined Laces
Trim seam allowance from the free edge of the entredeux. Place entredeux and insertion right side up with edges abutted.

Zigzag the two together, stitching into each hole of the entredeux and over the lace heading.

Sewing Gathered Fabric to Entredeux

Place entredeux and fabric right sides together, positioning the holes of the entredeux along the controlled area between the rows of gathering stitch. Stitch along the edge of the entredeux holes. Clean finish the raw edges. Press seam toward fabric. Remove visible basting.

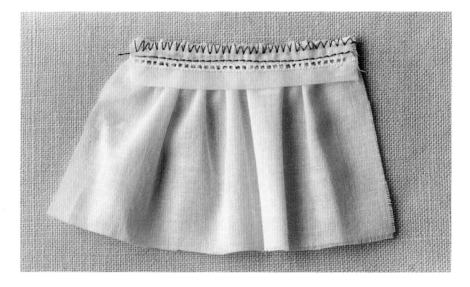

Attaching Puffing to Entredeux

Place the pieces right sides together, the entredeux holes just inside the rolled edge of the puffing. Stitch close to the holes. Press the seam open and trim the entredeux seam allowance even with the edge of the puffing.

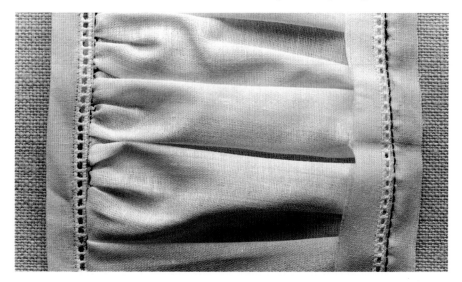

Gathering Lace

Pull a thread in the lace heading to gather lace to the desired measurement.

Gathering Embroidered Edging

Embroidered edging can be gathered by the same method used to gather fabric. Even up the raw edge of the trim. On the edging right side, stitch two rows of machine basting ¼ and ⅜ inch (.7 and 1 cm) from the raw edge. Pull bobbin threads to gather to desired measurement.

Joining Gathered Lace to Entredeux

Adjust gathers evenly. Stitch to the lace, using either method 1 or method 2 (pictured) for attaching lace to entredeux as described on page 32. Continue to adjust gathers as you work along; they will "travel."

Mitering Lace at Corners

For a square corner, place lace strips with right sides together, matching the design. Place a pin through the lace at a 45-degree angle.

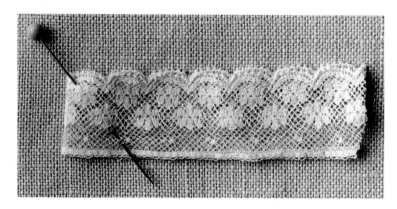

Open the corner to check that design is matched and angle of the miter is correct. Stitch from the right side along the pin placement line, then trim and overcast seam, or overcast stitch from the wrong side.

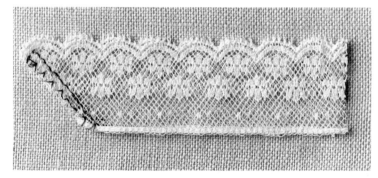

Press the seam open.

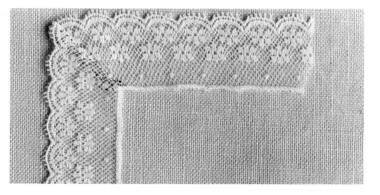

Attaching Lace to Fabric to Form Mitered Corners

With right sides together, pin lace to the fabric edge, with outer edge of lace heading ¼ inch (.7 cm) from fabric raw edge. At the corner, allow lace end to extend beyond fabric edge by the width of the lace. Baste lace in place, stitching along the inner edge of the heading and stopping at the point where stitching lines will meet at the corner.

Pin and baste lace to the adjacent fabric edge in the same way. Lift the first strip out of the way and stitch the second strip to the seamline intersection. Fold the lace outward, turn the seam allowances toward the fabric, and press.

To miter the corner of the lace: Fold the fabric corner diagonally, right sides together, and align the ends of the lace strips. Place a pin through the ends of the lace, exactly in line with the fabric fold.

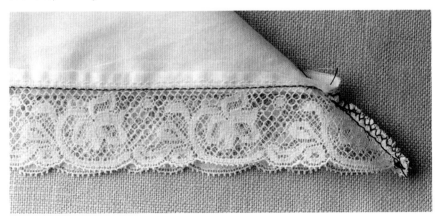

Open to check that the miter is correct. Stitch along the pin placement line. Trim seam allowance and overcast. On the right side, topstitch around the edge of the fabric close to the seamline if desired. If there is a tail at the corner, as in the photo, snip it off and whipstitch over the cut edges.

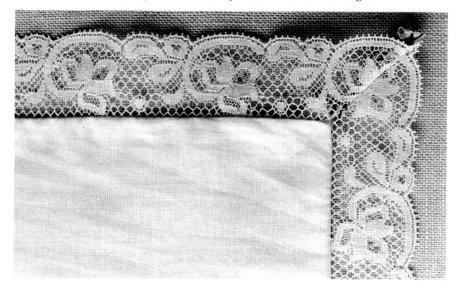

Applying Lace to a Rounded Corner
Clean finish or roll and whip fabric edges, rounding the corner. With right sides together, pin lace with the heading just inside the stitching or roll. Open out to check gathers. Stitch; press open. Topstitch if desired.

Joining Ends of Lace to Match Motifs

Allow enough extra lace to match pattern repeats. At each end where a join
will be necessary, allow extra length equal to the length of the pattern repeat.
To join the ends, place the two strips with right sides together, motifs
aligned. Pin the strips together, placing the pin at the center of a motif.

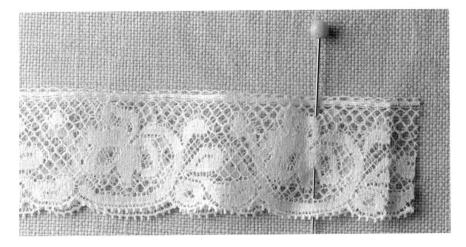

Open to the right side, check that the design is matched, and baste along the
fold. Stitch. Trim and overcast seam allowances.

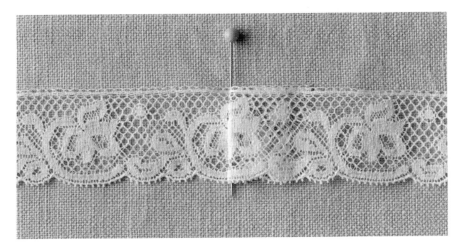

Joining and Finishing Ends of Embroidered Trim

Ends of embroidered trim can be sewn together with an overcast or serger
stitch, or with a French seam. Match motifs as for lace, above. Hem a free
end, such as on a ruffle, with a narrow double hem.

French Seams

This is an appropriate finish for seams on heirloom garments and on accessories where the wrong side may be visible. The raw edges are encased in the seam, preventing raveling and eliminating the necessity for overcasting, which can be too bulky with very fine fabrics.

Sew fabric edges with *wrong* sides together, using slightly less than half the total seam allowance. For example, if seam allowance is ½ inch (1.5 cm), stitch ³/₁₆ inch (6 mm) from the edge for this step. Trim away half the seam allowance.

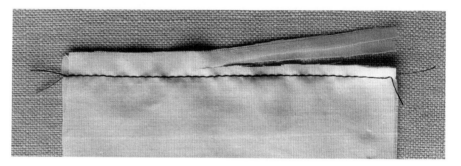

Press the piece flat, the seam allowances both in the same direction. Fold the piece with right sides together along the seamline; press. Stitch, using half the total seam allowance, encasing the raw edges.

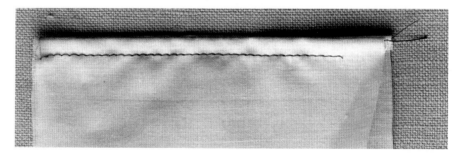

Bindings

Bias bindings provide a neat finish around armholes and neck edges. At a neck edge, binding of self fabric is more attractive than a facing that might show through the lace. To bind curved edges such as these, fabric for the binding must be cut on the bias so that the binding will conform to the curve without puckering.

Cut a bias fabric strip 1¼ (3 cm) wide and 1 inch (2 cm) longer than the edge to be bound. For a neckline binding, turn one end ½ inch (1 cm) to the wrong side. Place to the neck edge with right sides together and the folded end of the strip even with the finished neckline opening. Stitch, using ½ inch (1 cm) seam allowance. Trim seam allowances to ¼ inch (.5 cm). Fold bias to inside over the trimmed edge, then fold under the raw edge to just cover the previous stitching. Stitch in the ditch—the previous seamline—on the right side, or hand whip on the wrong side.

Apply an armhole binding in the same way. If the garment has a sewn shoulder seam, begin and end the binding at the underarm seam, folding under the overlapping end. If there are ribbon or lace straps at the shoulders, bind the underarm area before attaching them.

An alternative method for binding an edge is to use double fold bias tape made from garment fabric with a bias tape maker. Cut a fabric strip according to instructions with the tape maker, and form and press the strip. Fold the piece almost in half so that one edge is slightly short of the other, and press. Fold the strip over the garment edge with the shorter side of the tape strip to the garment right side. Stitch on the right side, close to the edge of the binding, catching the wrong side binding edge in the seam.

Plackets

A placket opening on a sleeve, neckline, or skirt can be finished quickly and neatly with a binding of self fabric. The instructions produce a narrow binding, appropriate for a sleeve or small neckline opening. For a wider binding, simply cut the fabric strip wider.

1. Mark the placket slash line on the garment, placing it on the grainline. Mark the end point.

2. Reinforce stitch around the end point with very short stitches before slashing. Cut along the slash line.

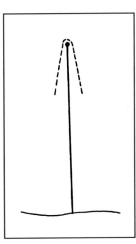

Before slashing the placket opening, stitch around the upper end with very short stitches to reinforce it.

3. Cut a fabric strip 1 inch (2.5 cm) wide and twice the length of the slash.

4. With the right side of the strip to the wrong side of the garment, stitch the two together. Use ¼ inch (.7 cm) seam allowance, less around the end point. Press seam allowances toward the binding.

5. Fold the binding to the right side of the garment along the stitching line. Fold under the binding raw edge so the fold just covers the previous stitching, and stitch close to the fold.

6. On the wrong side, fold the inner edges of the placket so they are even and stitch through both thicknesses of the placket at a slant as shown.

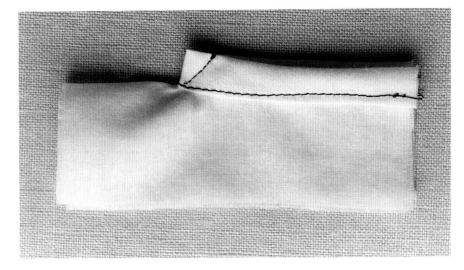

Tucks

Tucks can vary in size according to the nature of the project and the size of the area in which they will be placed. They can be spaced closely together or farther apart. Stitch close to the fold for a finer tuck, or make wider ones by stitching farther away.

Fold and stitch tucks precisely on the straight grain of the fabric. To ensure straight, parallel tucks, snip into the fabric edge at evenly spaced intervals and pull a thread from the center of each cut as shown. Crease the fabric, right side out, on the line created by the pulled thread. Stitch parallel with the crease.

3. Getting Started
WITH HEIRLOOM SEWING

The projects in this chapter were designed to introduce you to the materials and special construction techniques that typify heirloom sewing. If you have never worked with such light fabrics and laces, and if the sewing methods are unfamiliar to you, try a few of these quick-to-assemble projects. You will not only have several beautiful pieces of which you can be proud, but you will also have the skills and confidence to begin designing your own heirlooms.

Lace Scarves

THIS ACCENT PIECE IS A NON-FRILLY way to soften the lines of a tailored dress or jacket. The scarf can be worn looped over at the neckline. It can hang freely or be secured with a stickpin. Lengthen the scarf to hang to your waist, or make it thigh length for a long, flowing effect.

Make the scarf any length you like. To tuck into the neck of a blouse, 28 inches (72 cm) is about right. With a 45-inch (114-cm) length, the ends will reach to the waist. For the extra-long version, make it 60 to 72 inches (150 to 180 cm).

MATERIALS

The amount of lace edging and insertion you will need depends upon the desired finished length of the scarf. For the central panel, use insertion. You will need either one or two lengths, depending upon the width of the lace and the desired width of the scarf.

To determine the amount of edging you will need, first calculate the finished width of the scarf: the width of the planned central panel plus twice the width of the edging. Then calculate the finished length: the length of the central panel plus twice the width of the edging. For the total amount of edging, allow twice the finished width plus twice the finished length, plus enough extra to match the design at the four mitered corners.

CONSTRUCTION

Detailed instructions for each step are given in the heirloom sewing techniques section, beginning on page 20.

1. Prepare the laces and cut the central panel laces to size.

2. If more than one length of lace will be used for the central panel, assemble the panel.

3. Attach the edging around the central panel, mitering each corner and matching the pattern if possible.

A Variation

For a softer look, gather the lace edging at the corners of the central panel. Allow extra edging and follow the instructions for construction of the handkerchief, page 56.

Three-tiered Jabot

Tiers of exquisite embroidered edging or eyelet convert the basic office white shirt to an out-to-dinner confection! The jabot slips under the collar of a blouse and fastens in back with a snap. As an alternative, you might extend the neckband at each end to form ties.

MATERIALS

➤ ¾ yd (.7 m) embroidered edging, 5¼ inches (13.5 cm) wide
➤ Lightweight white fabric: one rectangle, 3½ by 5 inches (9 by 13 cm), for the foundation; for the neckband, one bias strip 2 inches (5 cm) wide, and in length the measurement of the blouse at the neckline seam plus 1½ inches (4 cm).
➤ Small snap

CONSTRUCTION

Detailed instructions for each step are given in the heirloom sewing techniques section, beginning on page 20.

1. Make the neckband. Turn under the ends of the bias strip ½ inch (1 cm) and press. Fold the strip in half lengthwise; press. Fold and press both long raw edges in to the center crease.

2. Hem both long edges of the foundation fabric with ¼ inch (.5 cm) double hems.

3. Cut edging into three equal strips. Hem the ends of each strip with a ¼ inch (.5 cm) double hem, or with a narrow blind hem.

4. Sew gathering stitch ¼ inch (.5 cm) from the raw edge of each piece. Gather each piece to 3 inches (7.5 cm).

5. Attach the edging tiers to the foundation, beginning at the bottom. Stitch the gathered edge of one edging piece to an unfinished edge of the foundation with right sides together and raw edges aligned, using ¼ inch (.5 cm) seam allowance. Overcast the seam allowances and press toward the foundation.

6. With wrong side of the tier to right side of the foundation, stitch the center tier across the foundation. Use an overcast stitch to overcast the tier raw edge at the same time. As an alternative, place a length of narrow ribbon over the tier raw edge and gathering threads. Turn under the ribbon ends and stitch.

7. Align the raw edge of the remaining tier with the raw edge of the foundation. Baste ¼ inch (.5 cm) from the edge.

8. Fold the pressed neckband strip over the raw upper edge of the completed piece, centering it. Beginning at one end of the strip, stitch the folded edges together and continue stitching across the tiers and to the other end of the band.

9. Sew snap section at each end of the strip.

A Variation

Make the tiers of fabric to match the blouse and edge them with lace or narrow eyelet. Plan the combined width of the fabric rectangles and edging to equal approximately 5¼ inches (13.5 cm). Cut three fabric rectangles and three strips of lace. Sew lace to the lower edge of each fabric piece and construct the jabot as described above.

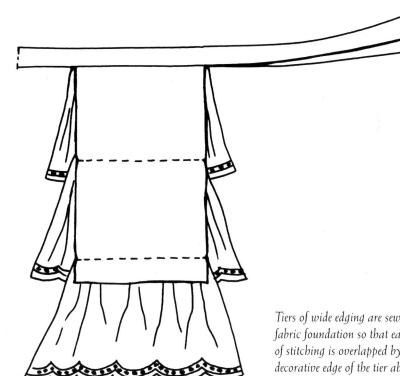

Tiers of wide edging are sewn to a fabric foundation so that each line of stitching is overlapped by the decorative edge of the tier above.

Sachets

Make them tiny to fill with pot-pourri or small treasures, or make them larger as an exotic alternative to everyday gift wrapping. These pretty bags offer a practical way to use up scraps of fabric and small bits of lace, to practice techniques, and to experiment with combinations of trims and tucks and ribbons.

MATERIALS

What you need will depend upon the desired finished size of the bag and the design you have in mind. The bags illustrated are approximately 4 by 6 inches (10 by 15 cm). Let the materials you have on hand inspire your own original creation! If you are short of ideas (or materials) at the moment, use the photograph for inspiration and to determine your shopping needs.

Design 1
Made of light blue Swiss batiste, entredeux joins the fabric to a narrow eyelet edging.

Design 2
Narrow eyelet edging trims floral print cotton lawn.

Design 3
Pale yellow fabric is edged with tiny French lace.

Design 4
Striped fabric overprinted with flowers, trimmed with cotton edging.

Design 5
Wide embroidered edging is used to make the bag itself. Cut a strip twice the desired width of the bag. Join the ends, right sides together, with an overcast stitch. Turn right side out and stitch across the lower (decorative) edge through both thicknesses. Stitch a narrow double hem around the top.

Design 6
Made like Design 5, using a different edging pattern.

Design 7
The bag is ecru linen. It is trimmed with lace edging joined to a coordinated beading/edging. Silk ribbon is woven through the beading.

CONSTRUCTION

To make the bags shown:

1. Cut two pieces of fabric to the desired dimensions.

2. With right sides together, stitch one side seam.

3. Cut trim(s) the width of the fabric piece.

4. Join trims, if necessary, and stitch to the upper edge of the bag as described in Chapter 2.

5. Fill, and tie closed with a 12-inch (30-cm) length of narrow ribbon.

Quick Camisole

In lightweight cotton, it's the coolest possible summer top. Make it up in dressier fabric with a wide lace ruffle and it can be a sensational topper for a black velvet skirt during the holiday season.

MATERIALS
➤ Fabric for the bodice, according to measurements
➤ Embroidered edging, 5¼ inches (13.5 cm) wide, according to measurements
➤ Narrow ribbon, according to measurements

MEASURING AND CUTTING
1. To determine width of fabric pieces for the front and back, use bust measurement and add 3 to 5 inches (8 to 13 cm) for seam allowances and ease. For length, measure from above the bust to the waist and add approximately 4 inches (10 cm) for ease and seam allowance. For front and back, cut two identical fabric rectangles, each this length and half the calculated bust measurement.

2. Shape the underarm at each side of both rectangles using the guide shown on page 123, or using a favorite pattern of your own.

3. For each underarm, cut a bias strip of fabric 1 inch (3 cm) wide to extend from upper front edge to upper back edge.

4. Cut two pieces of embroidered edging to fit the upper edges of the front and back.

5. Cut two pieces of ribbon, each the width of the front/back sections plus approximately 32 inches (82 cm) to tie across the shoulders. For the waistline, cut one piece, approximately twice the waist measurement to allow for ties.

CONSTRUCTION
Detailed instructions for each step are given in the heirloom sewing techniques section, beginning on page 20.

1. Stitch front and back together at the sides.

2. Stitch a bias strip around each underarm with right sides together and ½ inch (1 cm) seam allowance. Trim seam allowances and press toward bias. Fold bias to bodice wrong side along the seamline. Turn under bias raw edge, press, and stitch by hand or machine.

3. Finish the ends of both edging sections with narrow double hems.

4. Stitch the edging to each bodice upper edge with the right side of the edging against the wrong side of the bodice using ¼ inch (1 cm) seam allowance. Turn edging to the right side and press along the seamline.

5. To form the ribbon casing, stitch ½ inch (1.5 cm) from the upper edge.

6. To make the ribbon casing at the lower edge, turn 1 inch (2.5 cm) to the wrong side; press. Turn under the raw edge ¼ inch (.5 cm); press.

7. Mark placement for two buttonholes at center front on the right side. Space them approximately 1 inch (2.5 cm) apart, with the lower end approximately ¼ inch (.5 cm) above the pressed lower edge of the bodice. Work buttonholes slightly longer than the ribbon width.

8. Stitch the casing, stitching close to the inner fold and again close to the fold at the lower edge.

Camisole Variation
Instead of embroidered edging, use a piece of self fabric for the ruffle and trim it with lace. Attach the lace to the fabric first, then follow the steps above.

Nightgown Variation
For a pretty summer nightgown, just lengthen the camisole! You will probably want to cut the fabric wider, too, to allow more ease. The combined width of the front and back should equal the hip measurement plus the desired amount of ease.

Ascot

A very feminine ascot provides an attractive accent for a suit or blouse. It can be as dressy or tailored as the fabric used to make it. Our version is handkerchief linen; soft floral printed challis would make a nice alternative for cool weather wear.

Instructions are for a finished piece approximately 8 inches (20 cm) wide and 68 inches (172 cm) long. The length can be varied as you wish, of course.

MATERIALS
➤ Fabric, two pieces, 32 inches (81 cm) long and 6 inches (15 cm) wide, cut from the straight grain of the fabric
➤ Insertion lace, 1 inch (2.5 cm) wide, approximately 1⅛ yards (1.05 m)
➤ Edging lace, 5⅜ yards (4.95 m)

CONSTRUCTION
Detailed instructions for each step are given in the heirloom sewing techniques section, beginning on page 20.

1. With the pattern, lightly trace the point and lace placement at one end of each fabric section. *Note to serger users:* If desired, overcast outer edges of the pieces with a narrow stitch, then attach laces as instructed below.

2. Join the fabric sections. Abut the unmarked ends with right sides up. Center a piece of lace along the join and straight stitch along both headings.

3. Zigzag over the stitching lines.

4. On the wrong side, carefully trim the fabric close to the stitching.

5. On each marked end, place lace insertion along the placement lines, overlapping at the point.

6. Straight stitch just inside the lace headings, leaving the bottom strip free at the intersection.

7. Cut the point at each end of the ascot.

8. With right sides together, place edging along each diagonal edge, with the heading of the lace ¼ inch (.5 cm) in from the fabric edge. Overlap the lace ends at the point and allow them to extend beyond the fabric on all sides by the width of the lace.

9. Straight stitch the edging just inside the heading. Miter the corner at the point.

10. Zigzag over the straight stitching using a stitch width that just covers the lace heading.

11. Stitch lace edging along each side in the same way, mitering the points as before.

12. Turn lace right side out and press.

13. Topstitch close to the seamline all the way around. If fabric edges are unfinished, trim fabric seam allowance close to the stitching.

14. On the wrong side, carefully cut away fabric behind the applied lace strips, cutting close to the stitching lines.

Variations
This design can be adapted to suit all kinds of projects. Make it shorter and slightly wider to use as a place mat. Try it with heavier fabric and less delicate lace as a runner for the table or mantel, perhaps with a decorative tassel at each end.

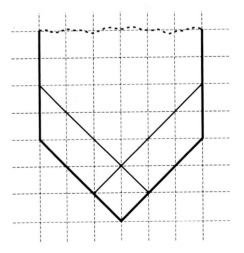

Position insertion strips with outer edges along the placement lines.

Lacy Handkerchief

Today, paper tissues have almost replaced the handkerchief. In times past, a handkerchief was not only functional, but decorative as well. Collections were kept in specially made cases and worn or carried in such a way as to show off the ornate handwork. Search through any antique shop and you will discover beautiful linen and batiste hankies richly embellished with lace and monograms.

An elegant contemporary handkerchief also can be displayed in the pocket of a blouse or tweed blazer. A handmade handkerchief is a thoughtful gift, especially appropriate as "something new" for a bride. Another way to showcase a beautiful handkerchief—old or new—is to tack its four corners to the front of a plain pillow cover.

MATERIALS

➤ Fine cotton batiste or very lightweight handkerchief linen, 9 inches (23 cm) square

➤ Lace edging, 1 to 3 inches (2.5 to 7.5 cm) wide, approximately 1½ yards (1.4 m)

CONSTRUCTION

Detailed instructions for each step are given in the heirloom sewing techniques section, beginning on page 20.

1. Prepare the fabric and lace.

2. Round off the corners evenly, then finish the fabric edges by rolling and whipping.

3. Mark the lace edging into fourths.

4. Sew the edging ends with right sides together, matching the pattern if possible.

5. With right sides together, pin the edging to the handkerchief, matching markings to corners. Pull a thread in the lace border to gather the lace around the corners.

6. Stitch the lace to the fabric with a close zigzag stitch the corners slightly. Press seam toward the fabric

4. Heirlooms At Home

Decorative accessories for your home—or that of a friend or loved one—offer unlimited opportunities for experimenting with enticing combinations of beautiful fabrics and trims. From pillows to place mats, upstairs or down, a touch of delicate lace or lavishly embroidered eyelet is a fitting complement to even the most contemporary decorating scheme.

Pillows

PILLOWS! PILLOWS! PILLOWS!
They offer a great opportunity to
display the beautiful fabrics and
trims you have collected. At the
same time, pillow covers allow you
to experiment with new designs
and combinations without worry-
ing about complicated construction techniques. There is always a
place to show off one more pillow.
Put away one or two to give as
gifts, too.

Pillow With Embroidered Ruffle

Tucks alternate with embroidered
beading to create a simple design
with plenty of detail. The wide ruffle lends a very feminine finish.

We have used white cotton batiste
fabric, but the design would be sensational, too, in a delicate floral print
or gingham. The embroidered beading has entredeux along both edges,
which eliminates the step of attaching a separate entredeux. The cover
has a back button closure so that it
can be removed for laundering.

MATERIALS
➤ Pillow form, 11 by 14 inches
(28 by 35.5 cm)
➤ ⅓ yd fabric
➤ 2½ yds (2.3 m) embroidered
beading with entredeux attached
➤ 2½ yds (2.3 m) ribbon, ⅛ inch
(3 mm) wide

➤ 4 yds (3.7 m) embroidered
edging, 5¼ inches (13.5 cm) wide

CONSTRUCTION
Detailed instructions for each step
are given the heirloom sewing
techniques section, beginning on
page 20.

Pillow Cover Front
1. For the tucked sections, cut six
fabric rectangles, 3 by 12 inches
(7.5 by 30.5 cm).

2. Fold each piece in half lengthwise. On a 3 inch (7.5 cm) edge,
snip the fabric edge ½ inch
(1.3 cm) each side of the center
fold to mark tuck foldlines. Pull a
thread at each snip. On the fabric
right side, crease along the line
made by the pulled thread and
stitch ⅛ inch (3 mm) from the fold.
Press. Repeat for all six rectangles.

3. Sew beading between each
pair of fabric strips, lining up
design of the beading. Thread ribbon through the beading strips.

4. Trim edges neatly to 12 by 15
inches (30.5 by 38 cm), maintain-
ing the rectangular shape.

Pillow Cover Back
1. Cut two pieces of fabric 10 by
12 inches (25.5 by 30.5 cm).

2. Fold one 12 inch (30.5 cm)
side of each piece 1 inch (2.5 cm)
to the wrong side, then 1 inch
(2.5 cm) again. Press.

3. Overlap the hemmed edges of
the sections and match to the
front. Make a buttonhole in the
overlapping hem and sew a button
in the corresponding position on

hem of the other section. Baste the sections together across the ends.

Ruffle

1. Join ends of the edging, right sides together. Mark into fourths.

2. Stitch two rows of gathering stitch, ¼ inch and ½ inch (.5 and 1 cm) from raw edge.

3. Draw up gathering threads to fit ruffle to cover front, matching marks to corners. Distribute gathers evenly, allowing more fullness at corners. Pin ruffle to top with right sides together. Baste around all sides, stitching along inner gathering line. Check gathers.

4. Place right side of cover back against right side of front, the ruffle between. Stitch from the front, following the basting line. Turn and press.

Neckroll Pillow

As tempting as it might be to use this pillow just for decoration, it really is meant to be functional. An inner cover contains the stuffing so the outer cover can be slipped off to wash.

Construction of this pillow illustrates an unusual heirloom sewing technique—attaching a combination of eyelet beading, narrow edging, and wide edging to a single seam allowance on each side of the center. The pillow can be enhanced with any combination of laces, trims and tucks that you desire. Add an embroidered monogram or appliqued motif to the central panel to personalize your design if you like.

Our pillow is 18 inches (46 cm) long, but the size can be varied.

MATERIALS

➣ Polyester batting, 18 by 45 inches (46 by 115 cm), or size needed for desired finished pillow size

➣ Fabric for outer cover, 24 by 18 inches (61 by 46 cm); and piece for central strip, 6 by 18 inches (15 cm by 46 cm)

➣ Fabric for inner cover, same amount as for outer cover

➣ Embroidered beading, 1 yard (.95 m)

➣ Embroidered edging, 5¼ inches (13.5 cm) wide, 1 yard (.95 m)

➣ Embroidered edging, 2½ inches (6.5 cm) wide, 2 yards (1.85 m)

➣ Ribbon, ¼ inch (.7 cm) wide, 3 yards (1.85 m)

CONSTRUCTION

Detailed instructions for each step are given in the heirloom sewing techniques section, beginning on page 20.

Inner cover

1. Stitch the 24 inch (61 cm) sides of fabric with right sides together to form a tube. Clean finish the seam.

2. To make a ribbon casing at each end, stitch a ½ inch (1 cm) double hem, leaving an opening. Insert an 18 inch (46 cm) length of ribbon in each.

3. Roll batting and insert into inner cover. Add or take out batting, if necessary, to fit cover. Draw up and tie ribbons.

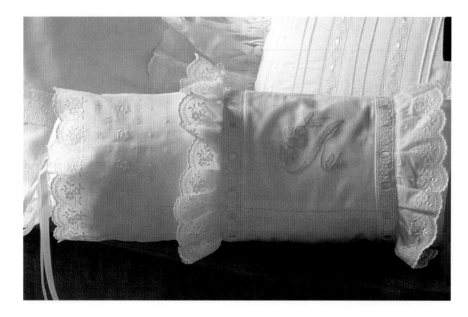

Outer cover

1. Stitch beading/entredeux to each long edge of the central strip with right sides together and stitching close to the holes of the entredeux. Press open, seam allowances toward center.

2. Cut 2½ inch (6.5 cm) eyelet strip in half. Gather each to the length of the central panel, and stitch, right sides together, to the other edge of the beading/entredeux. Press the stitching, but don't press open yet.

3. Cut wide edging in half. Place right side down over the narrower edging, raw edges aligned as shown. Stitch along the previous stitching line. Fold both layers of edging to the right side and press.

4. With both pieces right side up, center the panel at the center of the cover, ends aligned with the long sides of the cover. Baste across the ends.

5. Stitch the long edges together and make ribbon casings at the ends as for the inner cover.

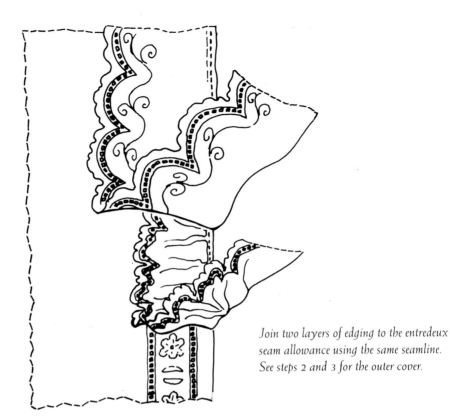

Join two layers of edging to the entredeux seam allowance using the same seamline. See steps 2 and 3 for the outer cover.

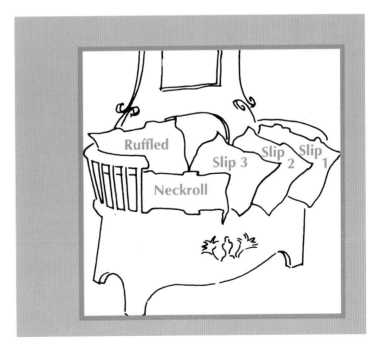

Chintz Neckroll Pillow

A simplified version of the neckroll pillow described on the preceding pages, the flowery chintz fabric needs little additional decoration. The trims are sewn flat onto the cover.

MATERIALS
➤ Poly batting, as for the neckroll pillow on page 60, or purchased pillow form
➤ Fabric for outer and inner covers, as for the neckroll pillow
➤ Narrow ribbon, 2 yards (1.85 m), for ends
➤ Wide ribbon, 1 yd (.95 m), or twice cover circumference
➤ Wide eyelet edging, 1 yd (.95 m), or twice cover circumference

CONSTRUCTION
Detailed instructions for each step are given in the heirloom sewing techniques section, beginning on page 20.

1. If a purchased pillow form is used, measure the circumference of the pillow, and add 1 inch (2 cm). Measure from the center of one end to the center of the other, and add 2 inches (4 cm) for hems. Cut fabric for inner and outer covers to these measurements.

2. Make the inner cover as for the neckroll pillow, above.

3. Cut edging in half and position the pieces, right side up, on

the outer cover section, the ends at the long edges of the cover and the decorative edges toward the ends of the cover. Space the strips so that the decorative edges will be 4 inches short of the ends of the pillow. Cut wide ribbon in half and position between the edging strips and overlapping the raw edges by ¼ inch (.5 cm). Stitch along both long edges of each ribbon and baste across the ends.

4. With right sides together, stitch the long edges of the cover.

5. At each end, stitch a ½ inch (1 cm) double hem for the ribbon casing, leaving an opening to insert the ribbon.

Pillow Slips

Once you start to think about them, you will invent dozens of ways to personalize pillow cases with trims and embellishments in every sort of combination. The designs shown here suit a range of pillow sizes, and can be adapted for use with purchased pillow slips too. For deserving friends, there could hardly be a more thoughtful special-occasion gift.

The covers shown are sized to fit a 12 by 16 inch (30.5 by 40.5) "boudoir" pillow. For other sizes, adjust quantities of materials accordingly.

MATERIALS

For all styles, you will need:

➤ Pillow form, 12 by 16 inch (30.5 by 40.5)

➤ Fabric, two pieces 13½ by 16 inches (34 by 40.5 cm), for front and back

➤ Lace or embroidered trim(s) for lower edge, ¾ yd (.7 m)

Pillow Slip 1 (right)

➤ Lace insertion, lace edging, and entredeux, ¾ yd (.7 m) each

➤ Lace beading, 1¼ yd (1.15 m)

➤ Ribbon, ¼ inch (6 mm) wide, 2½ yds (2.3 m)

Pillow Slip 2 (center)

➤ Lace edging, 1 yd (.95 m)

➤ Lace beading and entredeux, ¾ yd (.7 m) each

➤ Ribbon, ¼ inch (6 mm) wide, 2 yds (1.85 m)

Pillow Slip 3 (left)

➤ Embroidered edging incorporating entredeux, ¾ yd (.7 m)

➤ Embroidered galloon, ⅔ yd (61 cm)

➤ Ribbon, ¼ inch (6 mm) wide, ½ yd (.5 m)

CONSTRUCTION

Detailed instructions for each step are given in the heirloom sewing techniques section, beginning on page 20.

1. For pillow 3, sew strips of galloon diagonally across the lower front corners of the case front before assembling the case.

2. Sew case front to back along one side with right sides together and ½ inch (1 cm) seam allowance.

3. Serge, overcast, or roll and whip case lower edge.

4. Assemble trims and attach to case lower edge. If desired, fold the fabric seam allowance toward the case and topstitch in place from the right side.

5. With right sides together, stitch the remaining side seam and across the end.

Laundry Bag

Hand washables and delicate garments can be kept separate from the regular laundry in their own attractive bag. The open front placket offers all sorts of decorating potential, and the bag can be completed in next to no time. It slips over a hanger to keep things in order.

MATERIALS

Measurements are for a standard hanger that measures approximately 17 inches (43 cm) across. For other sizes, adjust dimensions and materials accordingly.

➤ Fabric, two pieces, each 18 by 21 inches (45.5 by 53 cm)
➤ Ribbon for bow, ⅓ yd (.3 m)
➤ Trim, approximately 1 yd (1 m)

CONSTRUCTION

1. Using your hanger as a guide, shape the upper edge of the bag: trace around the upper edge of the hanger on the wrong side of the fabric and add ½ inch (1 cm) seam allowance. Cut the pieces.

2. For the front placket, fold one fabric piece in half lengthwise and crease. Mark the lower end of the placket 12 inches (30 cm) below the top on the crease.

3. Slash and bind the placket according to the instructions on page 41.

4. Apply decorative trim around the placket opening, mitering the lower corners.

5. With right sides together, stitch the bag front to bag back around all four edges. Overcast the seams; turn.

6. Tie the bow. Tack it at the placket opening about 1 inch (2.5 cm) down from the top of the placket to hold the placket closed and keep the hanger in place.

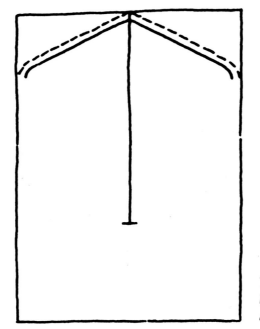

Trace the coat hanger upper edge onto doubled fabric. Add seam allowances at top and sides, and cut along the outer lines.

Picture Frame

There is always a need for one or two more picture frames, and they make great gifts for people who have everything. Highlight a cherished photo with a frame covered in fabric coordinated to the occasion—plaid for a Christmas picture, white for the wedding portrait, gingham or a tiny print for the photo of the new baby.

We used medium-weight linen to cover the frame.

MATERIALS
- Poster board, ⅛ inch (3 mm) thick: one piece the size of the frame; one piece for the backing, ¼ (.5 cm) smaller all around; one piece half to three-fourths the height of the frame and 2 to 3 inches (5 to 7.5 cm) wide for the stand
- Fabric, 3 inches (7.5 cm) longer and wider than the frame.
- Lining, for lightweight fabric, the size of the outer fabric
- Assorted trims and ribbons
- Liquid fray retardant
- White glue
- Craft knife

CONSTRUCTION
Detailed instructions for sewing laces and trims are given in the heirloom sewing techniques section, beginning on page 20.

1. For the outer frame, cut board to the desired dimensions and cut the opening in the center.

2. Baste lining to fabric, if needed. Fold fabric in fourths and make a small cut to mark the center. Carefully center the frame on the fabric and mark around the outer edge and around the opening. Add a 1-inch (2.5 cm) margin around outer edges and opening. Cut out the center section. Make a diagonal clip to within the frame's thickness of each inner corner. Apply a drop of fray retardant, if necessary, at each corner.

3. Position trims and stitch in place. As an alternative, trims can be glued after the fabric covering is in place.

4. Apply a thin layer glue to the edge and back of the frame around the opening. Position the frame right side down on the wrong side of the fabric and smooth the fabric around to the back. Glue the outer edges the same way, mitering corners or clipping away fabric to get them smooth.

5. If trims were not sewn, arrange them over the front of the covered frame and glue to the back.

6. Cut a V, slightly wider than the stand, in the back board where the upper end of the stand will be placed. Score across the upper end of the V and fold it outward.

7. Position the photo, checking from the front. Glue it in place.

8. Glue the smaller board onto the back, avoiding the area just above the V cut. Slip the stand in place.

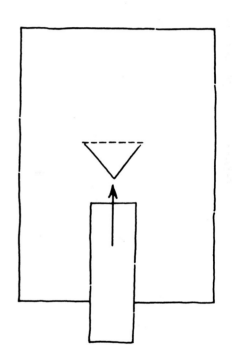

Cut a V in the backing, half to two-thirds of the way up, and slip the stand into the slot.

Place Mat and Napkin

What a lovely way to start the day! The simplicity of this design makes it most adaptable. It serves equally well for a single cheery mat and napkin on an individual tray, or for an elegant set of twelve to accompany the formal china. Neutral solid-colored fabrics, such as a traditional linen, can blend with an assortment of dishes. Bright floral chintz or gingham trimmed with eyelet can provide a colorful complement to a plain white place setting.

The place mat shown is 14 by 18 inches (35.5 by 46 cm). The napkin is 12 inches (30.5 cm) square, a good size for informal meals and luncheon settings. An 18 to 20 inch (46 to 51 cm) napkin is more often used for dinner and more formal meals. We have used lace edging around the mat and napkin, and a strip of matching insertion placed diagonally across one corner of each piece.

MATERIALS
➤ Fabric, according to number and size of mats and napkins
➤ Lace edging and insertion, according to measurements.

CONSTRUCTION
Detailed instructions for each step are given in the heirloom sewing techniques section, beginning on page 20.

Place Mat

1. Cut the fabric, pulling a thread to ensure each edge is perfectly straight.

2. Position insertion diagonally across a corner, approximately 4 inches (10 cm) from the corner. Stitch along both sides.

3. With right sides together and raw edges aligned, position lace edging along each side of the mat, allowing extra length at the ends to miter corners (see page 37).

4. Clean finish the seam allowances, press toward the mat, and topstitch.

Napkin

1. Cut the fabric 1 inch (2 cm) larger in length and width than the desired finished size of the napkin.

2. Add the lace insertion as for the place mat.

3. Hem the edges with ¼ inch (.5 cm) double hems.

Lampshade Cover

Toss this quick cover over a plain shade to add enchantment to the room. It is simply a circle trimmed with lace edging. Ribbon, woven through lace beading, secures the top opening and allows for minor adjustment to the cover length.

MATERIALS

Quantities will be determined by the measurements of your shade.

➤ Fabric, lightweight and translucent

➤ Lace beading, 2 inches (5 cm) longer than the upper circumference of the cover

➤ Ribbon, ¼ inch (.7 cm) wide and 18 inches (46 cm) longer than beading

➤ Lace edging, four times the length of the fabric

MEASURING AND CUTTING

1. To determine the width of fabric that will be needed, measure from the lower edge, up the shade, and across to the center of the opening as shown above right. Double this measurement, and add 1 inch (2 cm) for seam allowances.

Because the cover cannot be pieced inconspicuously, fabric width must be at least this measurement.

2. Use this same measurement for fabric length.

3. Fold the fabric in half lengthwise, then in half crosswise. Start-

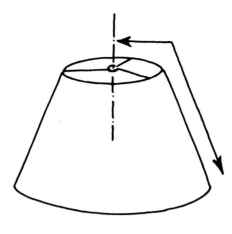

Measure shade to determine fabric length.

ing along one edge, measure from the point where the folds intersect by the amount determined in step 1. Mark the point. Continue measuring from the corner across to the other edge as shown, creating a curved line to represent the lower edge of the cover.

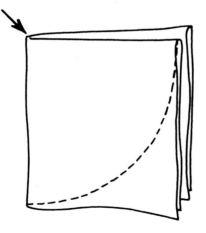

To establish the cover lower edge, measure from the corner and mark at approximately ¾-inch (2-cm) intervals.

4. Measure across the top opening in the shade. Using half that measurement, measure again from the folded corner of the fabric and mark another curved line to represent the upper edge of the cover.

5. Try the fabric on the shade to check the fit. Re-fold it, and cut the upper and lower edges.

CONSTRUCTION

Detailed instructions for each step are given in the heirloom sewing techniques section, beginning on page 20.

1. Position lace edging around the outer edge of the circle, right sides together, with raw edges even. Pull a thread in the lace heading to ease around the curved edge. Stitch. Clean finish seam allowances and press toward the fabric. Topstitch.

2. Stitch beading around the upper edge of the cover.

3. Thread the ribbon through and place on the shade to adjust the fit.

5. Heirlooms to Wear

Clothes and accessories designed around delicate fabrics and trims adapt very well to contemporary styles and requirements, and at the same time provide a note of elegance that today's fashions often lack. The ideas offered in this chapter are just a sampling of the way in which heirloom materials can blend with current trends.

How VERSATILE A SIMPLE PATTERN can be!
A basic top, worn under the suit jacket
on Monday or over a pair of comfortable
khakis on Saturday, takes on a new personality with the addition of pretty trim-
mings.

At right, the blouse front is made up of
three panels, joined together with wide
entredeux. Entredeux was used in the
sleeve seam, too; a technique that works
well with this pattern, since the dropped
shoulder has a nearly flat sleeve cap that
requires little easing.

The version at left is a bit dressier with its front
panels of floral-patterned eyelet insertion. The
sleeves were cut from wide edging in the same
eyelet pattern.

A Basic Blouse

A blouse with uncomplicated lines and a minimum of construction detail allows for all sorts of embellishment. The addition can be as simple as a strip of lace insertion down each side of the front or the creation of a yoke seam with entredeux in the seamline, or it can be very elaborate, as shown in some of the photographs on the following pages. There are lots of ideas for you to try, or to inspire your own combinations.

Use our pattern (page 123–125) as the basis for your designs, or use your own favorite. This one has a faced neckline and it buttons down the back. The long sleeves are gathered slightly at the shoulders and gathered onto two-piece cuffs. It is cut for a traditional fit.

We chose lightweight linen in a go-with-everything ivory shade for this model. Other soft, light fabrics would work equally well: cotton lawn or batiste, wool or wool and cotton challis, silk crepe de chine or lightweight broadcloth.

MATERIALS
- Fabric, for the blouse: 45 inch (115 cm) fabric without nap or one-way design, 2 yards (1.85 m) for sizes P and S; 2¼ yards (2.1 m) for other sizes
- Lightweight interfacing for neck facing and cuffs, or use self fabric
- Buttons, approximately ½ inch (1.3 cm), 7 for back and 4 for cuffs

CUTTING
1. Enlarge and cut out the pattern pieces on pages 123–125.

2. Fold fabric in half lengthwise, right side out. Lay out pattern pieces right side up to cut. Cut two strips for sleeve placket binding, 5¼ by 1½ inches (13.5 by 4 cm)

3. Cut interfacing for neck facing and cuffs

CONSTRUCTION
Use ⅝ inch (1.5 cm) seam allowances unless instructed otherwise.

Neckline and back facings
1. Baste or fuse interfacing to wrong side of neck facing sections.

2. Stitch front to back facing sections at shoulders. Press seams open.

3. Clean finish facing outer edge.

4. Stitch backs to front at shoulders. Press seams open.

5. Stay stitch neckline, stitching ⅛ inch (3 mm) from the seamline in the seam allowance.

6. With right sides together, stitch facing to neckline. Press seam allowances toward facing.

7. Understitch facing to seam allowances ⅛ inch (3 mm) from neck seamline. Trim seam allowance. Turn facing to inside; press.

8. Press a ½ inch (1.3 cm) hem along the inner edges of the back and neck facing. Blind stitch.

Sleeve and placket
1. Mark the placket slash line on each sleeve. Reinforce around the slash line and make the placket as described on page 41. Turn under front placket binding and baste in the seam allowance.

2. Loosen upper thread tension slightly and lengthen stitch slightly. With fabric right side up, sew a line of gathering stitch along the seamline of each sleeve cap. Stitch sleeve lower edges the same way.

3. Stitch the lower 6 inches (15 cm) of each sleeve seam. Press; clean finish seam allowances.

Cuffs
1. Baste or fuse interfacing to the wrong side of two (outer) cuff sections.

2. On the remaining cuff sections, press the seam allowance to the wrong side along one long edge. Trim pressed seam allowance to ¼ inch (.7 cm).

3. With right sides together, stitch cuff sections together at ends

and unpressed long edge. Trim seam allowances, turn right side out, and press.

4. Right sides together, pin cuff to sleeve. Pull the bobbin thread to gather sleeve edge to fit. Stitch. Press seam allowances toward cuff; trim.

5. Pin pressed edge of cuff facing just over stitching. Whipstitch.

Sleeves and side seams

1. With right sides together, pin sleeve to armhole, matching at shoulders. Pull bobbin thread to gather sleeve cap to fit.

2. Stitch, then stitch again ⅛ inch (3 mm) away in seam allowance. Trim seam allowance and clean finish.

3. Stitch side seam and remainder of sleeve seam, matching seamlines at underarms. Clean finish seam allowances.

Finishing

1. Overcast or stitch a narrow hem around the lower edge.

2. Mark placement of buttonholes along back hem and work buttonholes. Work buttonholes on cuffs. Sew buttons in corresponding positions.

3. Adjust pressed hems in back facing edges to avoid button/buttonhole area. Whipstitch to back hems.

Lacy Front Inset

The addition of a front inset with narrow tucks and lace edging gives the basic blouse an entirely new personality. Wide edging is gathered into the seam at the lower edge of the cuffs for a dramatic effect. The design is an adaptation of a blouse found in the closet of an old estate. The original was sewn entirely by hand—this version goes together much more quickly.

MATERIALS

➤ Fabric, according to yardage for the basic blouse on page 75 or

for your own similar pattern.

➤ For the tuck panel, an additional piece of blouse fabric, or a compatible fabric, 8 inches (20 cm) square.

➤ Lace edging, 3½ inches (9 cm) wide, ¾ yard (.7 m) for front inset, 1 yd (.95 m) for cuffs, and 5/8 yard (.6 m) for the tie

➤ Lightweight interfacing for cuffs

CUTTING

1. For the blouse front, cut a fabric rectangle as long as the blouse front measured from the shoulder at the neckline to the lower edge, and 2 inches (5 cm) wider at each side than the blouse front. Mark a center front line on the piece.

2. Cut the cuff sections narrower, if desired, to allow for the width of the lace.

3. Replace the neck facing with a bias binding as described on page 40.

4. Cut remaining pieces as for the basic blouse or according to your pattern instructions.

CONSTRUCTION

Detailed instructions for the steps involving heirloom sewing techniques are found in Chapter 2, beginning on page 20.

Blouse front

1. Prepare the tuck panel as described on page 43. Mark three tuck foldlines ½ inch (1.3 cm)

apart on each side of center front. Stitch each tuck close to the foldline and press outward from center. Clean finish sides and lower edge of the piece.

2. Position the tuck panel on the blouse front block, matching centers. Baste.

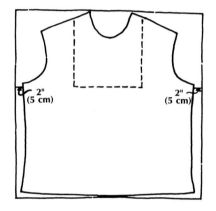

Cut a fabric rectangle for the blouse front. Form the shoulder pleats and add the embellishment, then cut to the pattern.

3. Position lace edging around the tuck panel, right side up, with the decorative edge inward, covering the edges of the tuck panel. Miter lower corners of the lace.

4. Reposition lace on the front and sew in place, stitching along the inner edge of the lace heading.

5. By hand or machine, stitch again just inside the scalloped edge of the lace to attach it to the tuck panel.

6. Make pleats at shoulders. On the right side, crease fabric along

the lengthwise grainline approximately 1 inch (2.5 cm) outside the lace and fold a 1-inch (2.5-cm) pleat toward the armhole. Press, extending creases below shoulder seamlines.

7. Position the pattern over the block, matching center front lines. Mark the cutting lines. Stitch just inside the marked lines and cut out the piece. On the wrong side, carefully trim away blouse fabric from behind the tuck panel and lace.

Cuffs

1. Baste interfacing to outer cuff sections. Press under seam allowance on one long edge of remaining cuff sections (facings).

2. Cut two pieces of lace edging one and one-half times the length of the cuff. Hem the ends.

3. Gather lace to fit long edge of cuff between seamlines.

4. Position lace on outer edge of outer cuff section, right sides together, aligning the inner edge of the lace heading with the cuff seamline. Baste.

5. Stitch cuff to facing, keeping outer edge of lace free.

Complete the blouse following the construction steps on pages 75–76. Instead of facing the neck edge, apply bias binding as described on page 40.

Tie

1. Cut a strip of fabric 4 by 10 ½ inches (10 by 26.5 cm).

2. Cut two pieces of edging 10 ½ inches (26.5 cm) long.

3. Stitch lace to long edges of fabric strip with right sides together. Clean finish seams and press toward fabric.

4. Stitch a narrow double hem at each end.

5. Cut a fabric strip 2 by 1 ½ inches (5 by 4 cm). Press long edges ¼ inch (.5 cm) to wrong side. Wrap tightly around center of bow and tack to back.

6. Tack to blouse at center front of neckline.

Tucks and Lace

Lightweight linen in a summery shade of periwinkle is dressed up with tucks and laces. On the blouse front, strips of tucked fabric alternate with lace insertion. The design is repeated horizontally on the sleeve with a trio of tucks above and below the lace insertion. A narrow, standing collar was added, and trimmed with gathered lace.

Instructions below apply to the basic blouse on page 75, but the design could be applied to any similar blouse pattern.

Materials

- Fabric for the blouse
- Lace insertion, approximately 3 yards (2.75 m)
- Lace edging, approximately 1⅜ yards (1.3 m)
- Buttons, for back and cuffs

Cutting

1. For the blouse front, cut a fabric rectangle as long as the blouse front measured from the shoulder at the neckline to the lower edge, and 2 or more inches (5 cm) wider at each side than the blouse front as shown in the drawing on page 78. Mark a center front line on the piece.

2. Cut a rectangle for each sleeve, the width of the pattern piece and approximately 2 inches (5 cm) longer.

3. For the collar length, measure the neckline around the seamline.

Add 1 inch (2 cm) for seam allowances. Cut two pieces on the bias, this length and 2 inches (5 cm) wide. Cut interfacing, or a piece of self fabric, this same size.

4. Cut remaining pattern pieces according to the basic blouse instructions, omitting the neckline facings.

CONSTRUCTION

Detailed instructions for the steps involving heirloom sewing techniques are found in Chapter 2, beginning on page 20.

Follow the steps below for the design changes for this blouse. Construct the blouse according to the instructions on page 75–76.

Blouse front

1. Center a strip of lace insertion, right side up on right side of fabric, at center front. Stitch along the inner edges of both lace headings.

2. Mark foldlines for three tucks on each side of the lace, spacing them ½ inch (1.3 cm) apart. Crease along the lines, stitch close to the folds, and press away from center.

3. Add another strip of lace insertion at each side of the tucked area.

4. Make three more tucks outside each of these lace strips.

5. Position the pattern over the block, matching center front lines. Mark the cutting lines. Stitch just inside the marked lines and cut out the piece.

Collar

1. Baste interfacing to the wrong side of one (outer) collar section. Trim interfacing seam allowances.

2. On the other collar section (the facing), turn the seam allowance on one long edge; press.

3. Use a strip of lace edging approximately one and one-half times the length of the collar. Hem the ends. Pull a thread from the heading to gather the lace to fit the collar edge.

4. Place lace to outer collar, right sides together, with the inner edge of the lace heading along the seamline. Baste.

5. Pin collar facing to outer collar, right sides together. Stitch ends and outer edge. Trim, turn, and press.

6. Stay stitch the blouse neckline and finish edges of back opening according to instructions for the basic blouse.

7. Pin the collar to the neckline with right sides together, clipping the neck edge as necessary. Stitch.

Sleeves

1. On each sleeve piece, mark a point slightly above the elbow and pull a crossgrain thread at that point to indicate the straight grain.

2. Center lace insertion over the marked line and stitch it in place.

3. Mark and stitch three tucks above and three below the lace, spacing and stitching them as for the front.

Cuffs

1. Baste interfacing to outer cuff sections. Press under seam allowance on one long edge of remaining cuff sections (facings).

2. Cut two pieces of lace edging one and one-half times the length of the cuff. Hem the ends.

3. Gather lace to fit long edge of cuff between seamlines.

4. Position lace on outer edge of outer cuff section, right sides together, aligning the inner edge of the lace heading with the cuff seamline. Baste.

5. Stitch cuff to facing, keeping outer edge of lace free.

Trimmed with Eyelet

Equally at home with jeans or a long velvet skirt, this crisp white blouse is trimmed with eyelet insertion, beading, and edging in two widths. The embellishment is far less complicated than it looks. Begin with the basic blouse, pages 123–125, or use a similar pattern of your own. The ruffle pattern is on page 123.

The "collar" is a piece of medium-width edging, joined to the blouse neckline along with a ruffle of gathered edging. The front ruffle is a strip of wide edging, tapered at the lower end and stitched in place at the shoulder.

The ruffle can be made to extend down the back as well—just make the same changes to the pattern back as to the front, and cut the edging twice as long. The blouse front pattern was slashed at a slight diagonal from shoulder to lower edge to provide the seam into which insertion and gathered edging are sewn.

Beading and medium-width edging are sewn into a seam cut across the sleeve at the elbow. At the cuff, medium edging is gathered onto insertion. If desired, the sleeve can be shortened to three-quarter length, the cuffs cut longer, and the plackets omitted.

The blouse instructions begin on page 75. This design could easily be adapted to any collarless blouse with a back opening.

MATERIALS
- Fabric for the blouse

For the front ruffles:
- Wide eyelet edging, 1½ yds (1.4 m)
- Eyelet insertion/entredeux, approximately 1⅜ yards (1.3 m)

For the collar:
- Medium width edging, one piece the length of the neckline, measured along the seamline, plus 1 inch (2 cm), and one piece one and one-half times this measurement

For the sleeve variation:
- Eyelet beading/entredeux, twice the sleeve pattern width
- Medium width eyelet edging, twice the sleeve pattern width
- Ribbon, ¼ inch (.7 cm) wide, 1½ yards (1.4 m)

For the cuff variation:
- Eyelet insertion/entredeux, twice the cuff pattern length
- Medium eyelet edging, three times the cuff pattern length

MARKING THE PATTERN
1. Make a copy of the front and sleeve pattern pieces to make the changes.

Mark placement lines for ruffles, taking into consideration the width of the edging. Place the lower ends of the ruffle approximately at the waistline.

2. For the front ruffle, draw a diagonal line on the pattern front piece for placement of the insertion and ruffle. Start approximately 2 inches (5 cm) from the neckline at the shoulder—or closer to the armhole if desired—and taper slightly toward center front at the lower edge. Allow for the width of the edging at the shoulder. If insertion will be used, cut the pattern along this line and adjust for width of insertion.

3. On the sleeve piece, draw a line across the pattern approximately 1 inch (2.5 cm) above the elbow and perpendicular to the lengthwise grainline.

CUTTING
1. Cut the central section of the blouse front, to the diagonal line on the pattern. Side sections will be cut after insertion has been attached.

2. Cut the back according to the basic pattern.

3. Cut trims for the collar as described in Materials, above.

4. Cut a fabric rectangle for each sleeve, the width and length of the pattern piece at the widest and longest points.

5. Cut two ruffles from wide edging according to the pattern on page 123. Place the scalloped edge along the straight line and curve the unfinished edge as shown. Cut two strips of insertion the length of the diagonal line.

6. Cut trims for the sleeve inset to the sleeve width at the marked line.

7. Cut trims for the cuff as described in Materials, above.

8. Cut bias strips long enough to bind each sleeve placket and ends of cuff trims.

9. Omit cuff and neckline facings.

CONSTRUCTION

Instructions for the variations are given here. For the basic blouse construction, see page 75. Details of heirloom sewing techniques are found in Chapter 2, beginning on page 20.

Blouse front

1. Sew insertion/entredeux along diagonal front edges. Use this piece and the pattern to cut side front sections, allowing for the width of the insertion.

2. Hem the wide end of each ruffle. Gather unfinished edges of ruffle sections as necessary to fit the diagonal line from shoulder *seamline* approximately to waistline, allowing more ease in the shoulder area.

3. With right sides together, baste ruffle to remaining edge of insertion/entredeux. Position a side section along the diagonal seamline with right sides together and the ruffle between. Stitch, clean finish seams, press.

Collar

1. Stitch backs to front at shoulders; press seams open. Stay stitch the neckline.

2. Finish ends of both edging sections.

3. Gather longer edging piece to fit neck seamline. Position on the neck edge, wrong side of ruffle to right side of blouse, and baste along the seamline.

4. With right sides together, stitch the other edging section to the neckline, clipping the neck edge as necessary. Trim and overcast seam allowances.

Sleeve and cuff

1. Cut the sleeve rectangles horizontally according to the marked

An elaborate combination of trims is used here to make up the entire sleeve. Very wide edging ends just below the elbow, overlapping a fabric panel with a central insertion/entredeux strip bordered by narrow edging. A second piece of wide edging forms the lower end of the sleeve, its decorative edge overlapping the fabric panel and its "upper" edge at the wrist, finished with narrow gathered edging.

line on the pattern. Attach beading to the cut edge of each upper section.

2. Place the edging, right side down, against the free edge of the beading. Stitch.

3. Place the lower sleeve section cut edge along the same edge of the beading, right sides together. Stitch along the previous stitching line. Clean finish seams; press.

4. Cut sleeve by the pattern.

5. Reinforce and slash the placket, but do not bind it yet.

6. Stitch and clean finish the lower 6 inches (15 cm) of the sleeve seam.

7. Gather sleeve lower edge to fit cuff.

8. Gather edging to fit cuff. Stitch, with right sides together. Clean finish seams.

9. Stitch cuff to sleeve, aligning unfinished ends with edges of placket opening.

10. Bind the placket and cuff ends as described on page 41. Work buttonholes or button loops on cuff fronts.

Simple Changes

A touch of heirloom trim can produce spectacular results with almost any simply constructed garment. Use your imagination!

For a quick and clever variation on the traditional cuff, replace it with wide embroidered edging. Here, a rather unusual colored eyelet is joined to the sleeve with entre-deux/insertion of the same design. Because there is no facing or interfacing, small button loops were used instead of sewn buttonholes. Narrow hems finish the ends of the cuff.

Wide lace edging outlines the front, lower edge, and sleeves to make a plain linen jacket extraordinary. Satin ribbon covers the stitching line, and porcelain rosebuds have replaced plain buttons down the front.

Lace-Edged Scarf

Lace and tweed are a classic team, each complementing the other. The ends of this graceful scarf are slightly on the bias so it will conform neatly to necklines and shoulder curves. Soft fabrics, fairly light in weight, work best for this design. Our model is made of the same lightweight linen used for the basic blouse on page 74.

MATERIALS

➤ Fabric, 45 inches (115 cm) wide, 1 yard (.95 m)
➤ Lace edging, 3 yards (2.75 m)

CONSTRUCTION

1. Enlarge the pattern on page 123 and cut fabric.

2. Clean finish edges of the scarf.

3. Apply lace edging, beginning at the center of the inner neck edge. With lace and fabric right sides together, align lace heading with inner stitching of the fabric edge finish. Pull a thread in the heading to ease lace around curves, and leave extra lace to join at the ends. Baste in place.

4. Join the lace ends with an overcast seam.

5. Press, turning seam allowance toward fabric. Topstitch.

Summer Nightgown

Make it short and abbreviated for humid midsummer nights, or make it long and flowing for times when you want to feel absolutely elegant. This one is cool cotton, trimmed with the whitest eyelet. The style is so adaptable that it would work just as beautifully in batiste, gingham, or soft cotton challis—each creating an entirely different look.

The gown fits a range of sizes. To widen across the top, or yoke, cut facings wider and assemble laces to fit the facings.

MATERIALS
➤ Fabric for gown, 45 inches (115 cm) wide, two lengths (see step 1, below)
➤ Fabric for facings, two pieces 6 by 12 inches (15 by 30.5 cm)
➤ Assorted laces and trims to make up front and back yokes, or for back yoke use fabric piece 6 by 12 inches (15 by 30.5 cm)
➤ Ribbon for ties, 1½ inches (4 cm) wide, 2 yards (1.85 m)
➤ Lace edging for hem, if desired, 2½ yards (2.4 m)

CONSTRUCTION
Detailed instructions for the steps that involve heirloom sewing techniques are found in Chapter 2, beginning on page 20.

1. For the gown front and back, measure from above the bust to the desired finished length. Add hem allowance if lower edge will not be trimmed with lace.

2. Sew fabric lengths together at the sides.

3. With seams at the sides, cut armholes using the armhole guide on page 123. Bind edges with bias strips of fabric as described on page 40.

4. Gather upper edge of front and back to fit between seamlines (½ inch or 1.3 cm from each end) of yoke front and back. Sew yoke right side to front/back wrong side. Clean finish seams and press toward yoke.

5. Cut ribbon into four pieces. Position a ribbon just inside the seamline at the outer edge of each yoke section, on the yoke right side, ribbon end aligned with yoke upper edge. Baste.

6. Join laces or embroidered trims for the outer yoke sections. Join horizontal strips to the size of the yoke facing, using edging along the lower edge and allowing it to extend just below the yoke facing/skirt seamline.

7. Position yoke to facing with right sides together. Stitch at the sides and across the top, keeping ribbon ends free. Trim, turn right side out, and press.

8. For a fabric back yoke, clean finish the lower edge. Turn ¼ inch (.7 cm) to wrong side. Press, and topstitch.

9. Hem lower edge, or attach lace.

Skirts and Petticoats

Either one is a perfect candidate for adornment with heirloom materials and techniques. Wide edging suits them especially well. Rows of tucks can be charming around a hemline. Beading, sewn in just above the hemline and threaded with a contrasting ribbon, is a simple and elegant way to add a new detail to your faithful old skirt pattern.

Choose a pattern with the lower edge cut straight on the fabric crossgrain, especially if tucks will be added. It is easiest to add embellishments to a flat piece. Stitch one side seam—both if there is a center back seam—so you will have the entire skirt as a single piece upon which to work. If tucks are used, add them to each piece before sewing seams

Any skirt pattern that is fairly wide at the lower edge and that has just a few darts or pleats at the waist can be used for a petticoat. Eliminate darts or pleats and re-shape the upper edge. Add a casing for a narrow ribbon to draw in waistline fullness. If necessary, add a bound placket at the back.

Choose lightweight cotton fabric, such as batiste or lawn. For the ruffle at the bottom, buy wide edging, one and one-half to two times the circumference of the skirt.

Join the ends of the edging. Mark the edging and the lower edge of the skirt in fourths. Gather the edging to the skirt edge and stitch with right sides together. (Refer to Chapter 2 for detailed instructions for these techniques.)

A simple skirt, very elegant in fine linen, features a strip of entredeux just above the inner edge of the hem.

A plain pleated skirt (opposite) acquires a feminine air with the addition of a few rows of tucks and wide eyelet edging around the bottom. Choose a fabric that blends well with the ground fabric of the eyelet; this linen is a perfect choice.

A petticoat richly edged with Swiss embroidery should be allowed to show just a little.

A very old piece of fabric, found in a back corner of an antique shop, features exquisite eyelet patterns worked on the softest linen imaginable. It was too pretty to store away in a trunk, so was quickly converted into a most feminine skirt. A bound placket was added at the back waistline. The waist edge was gathered onto a wide ribbon with the ribbon ends left long enough to tie.

Antique Camisole

Don't hesitate to take design ideas from vintage garments! When this camisole was made, women seem to have had more time to devote to the creation of beautiful garments. The camisole is hand sewn in the softest silk and lace imaginable.

It inspired this modern interpretation—far less costly and time-consuming to put together. Wide ribbon and lace insertion alternate, creating vertical stripes around the lower section, with narrower lace and ribbon placed horizontally to make the yoke.

Use a basic tank top pattern as a guide. Eliminate the seam allowances and widen by an inch or two at center front and center back. For length, measure from the shoulder over the bust to the waist, and add approximately 2 inches (5 cm) ease.

On a large sheet of paper, trace around the pattern to create a diagram as shown on page 94. Use the diagram to calculate the yardage of lace and ribbon you will need, and to determine their placement.

MATERIALS

For the lower section:
- Lace insertion, 1½ inches (4 cm) wide
- Ribbon, 1½ inches (4 cm) wide

For the yoke:
- Lace insertion, approximately 1 inch (2.5 cm) wide
- Ribbon, approximately 1 inch (2.5 cm) wide. As an alternative, you may use the same ribbon and lace width as was used for the lower section, or make the yoke entirely of insertion.
- Narrow lace edging, for the armholes and neckline
- Lace beading, for the armholes and neckline
- Ribbon, ¼ inch (.7 cm) wide,

about twice the length of the beading.

➤ Clear snaps
➤ Fabric scrap to match color of lace

CONSTRUCTION

Detailed instructions for the heirloom sewing techniques are found in Chapter 2, beginning on page 20.

1. For the lower section, cut ribbon and insertion as needed for your pattern. Sew the strips together, alternating the two. Begin at the left side with ribbon and end at the right with lace.

2. Make up the yoke section, alternating lace and ribbon. Allow ends to extend ½ inch (1.5 cm) or so at the center front edges.

3. Use the pattern as a guide to trim edges evenly, leaving the extensions at yoke center front.

4. Attach the yoke to the lower section. Overcast the ends of the yoke center front extensions. Turn to the wrong side along the center front line and whipstitch in place.

5. Stay stitch all raw edges, stitching close to the edge.

6. Sew beading, then narrow edging, around neckline and armholes. Thread ribbon through the beading.

7. Clean finish the lower edge. Turn to the inside and hem. If desired, use the hem as a casing for a narrow ribbon to draw in the waistline. The lower edge might be finished instead with beading and edging.

8. At the front, overlap lace edge over ribbon edge and position snaps. As an alternative, sew lengths of narrow ribbon opposite each other on the front edges and tie bows to close the front.

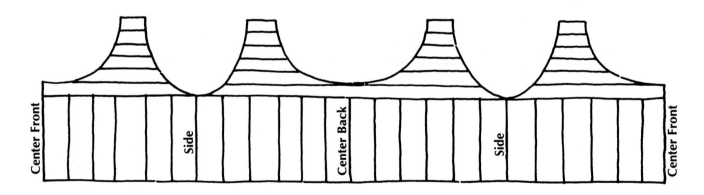

Make a diagram from your pattern to determine yardages for lace and ribbon and to plan the layout.

Lace Collar and Jabot

A lace collar with its own jabot goes together quickly and makes a luxurious accent piece to soften the lines of a jacket or plain blouse. Wide lace edging is gathered and layered onto a fabric foundation, its upper edge bound with bias-cut fabric.

MATERIALS

➤ Wide lace edging, 1½ yds (1.4 m)

➤ Fabric, to match lace, a bias strip, 1½ inches (4 cm) wide and in length the neckline measurement plus 2 inches (5 cm); a rectangle 3½ by 5 inches (9.5 by 12.5 cm).

➤ Clear snap or small button

CONSTRUCTION

1. To make a foundation for the lace tiers, hem the long sides and lower edge of the fabric rectangle with a narrow double hem, or serge the edges.

2. Cut two 12-inch (30-cm) pieces from the lace strip. Stitch a narrow double hem at each end of each piece.

3. On the longer lace strip, pull a thread in the heading and gather it to a length 2 inches (5 cm) shorter than the bias strip. Center the fab-

ric foundation right side up behind the gathered lace, upper raw edges aligned.

4. Stitch the gathered lace and foundation to the bias strip, lace and bias with right sides together. Press seam allowances toward bias. At each end, fold the strip ½ inch (1 cm) to the wrong side; press.

5. For the jabot tiers, gather the remaining lace strips to the width of the foundation. Position one tier right side up on the foundation right side, just above the lower edge. Center the second tier above

the first so each heading is over-lapped. Stitch each tier to the foundation with a zigzag stitch.

6. Fold the raw edge of the bias strip ¼ inch (.7 cm) to the wrong side, then fold in again so outer fold overlaps stitching line along collar. Stitch close the inner folded edge.

7. Sew a snap or button and loop to fasten the ends.

A Nightgown for All Seasons

A lace-topped gown made in the French handsewing tradition, this adaptable style allows for the most imaginative combinations of laces and trims you can dream up. The gown can be made any length you wish, with sleeves or without.

A jewel-necked blouse pattern with sleeves and a back opening, such as the one on page 75, can easily be modified to make the gown. You may wish to use a larger size for more wearing ease. Then use the pattern to experiment with an arrangement of laces that pleases you.

PREPARING THE PATTERN

Trace the front, back, and sleeve pattern pieces to preserve the original.

1. Determine placement of the yoke seamline, just above the bustline or as you prefer. Draw a horizontal line on the front and back at that point, perpendicular to the center front and center back lines. The gown will be open along the center back of the yoke.

2. Cut along the horizontal lines for the yoke front and back patterns. Save the lower sections; the armhole will be used as a cutting guide later. To cut fabric, add seam allowances along the cut edges.

3. The sleeve can be widened for wearing ease. Draw a line from shoulder to lower edge, parallel with the grainline. Draw a horizontal line across the piece perpendicular to this to help with realignment of the pieces.

4. Cut along the vertical line and separate the halves by an inch or so, or as desired. The excess at the cap will be gathered around the shoulder when the gown is constructed.

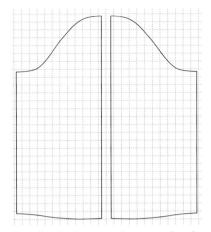

To widen the sleeve, cut the pattern lengthwise from shoulder to lower edge. Separate the pieces by the desired amount.

5. If your pattern has a cuff at the lower edge, straighten the lower edge line.

6. Determine the sleeve length, taking into account the width of the lace trim you will add. Check that both sides of the sleeve are equal in length.

7. On a large sheet of paper, use the pattern piece as a guide and draw a rectangle approximately 1 inch (2.5 cm) longer than the front yoke pattern measured from the shoulder at the neckline to the yoke lower edge, and 1 inch (2.5 cm) wider than the entire front at the widest point.

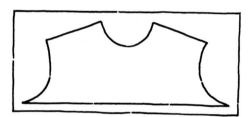

Assemble the laces in the form of a rectangular block slightly longer and wider than the pattern piece. Use the pattern to mark the cutting line, stitch just inside the marked lines, and cut out the piece.

8. Draw a rectangle in the same way to represent half the back yoke, to the center back line. Do not add center back seam allowance.

9. Use these blocks to determine quantities of laces or trims needed, and to plan their arrangement.

Materials

➤ Fabric, for the skirt and sleeves. For the skirt, use two lengths of 45-inch (115-cm) fabric.
➤ Fabric for back facings, neckline binding, and as armhole binding for a sleeveless gown. Use the gown skirt fabric, or a color to blend with the laces.
➤ Laces, trims, and ribbon according to your design for the yoke and sleeve edging
➤ Lace edging, one and one-half times the width of the yoke front and back lower edges. For a sleeveless gown, you will also need edging three times the length of the total yoke armhole measurement.
➤ Lace edging, if desired, for the gown hemline
➤ Small button

Construction

Detailed instructions for the heirloom sewing techniques are found in Chapter 2, beginning on page 20.

Front Yoke

1. Cut strips of lace the length of the yoke block. Take care to line up lace patterns and beading holes across the block. Stitch the strips together to cover the width of the block.

2. Place the pattern piece over the block. Chalk mark the outline of each half. Stitch just inside the lines and cut out the piece.

3. Cut a strip of lace edging one and one-half times the width

across the yoke lower edge. Gather it to fit. With right sides together, align the inner edge of the lace heading with the seamline. Stitch.

Back Yoke

1. Assemble the back yoke sections in the same way. At the center back line, allow lace to extend beyond the line by ¼ inch (.5 cm) on each side. Mark seamlines according to step 2, above.

2. To face the center back edges, cut two strips of fabric, ½ inches (3 cm) wide and the length of the yoke at center back.

3. Stitch a strip to each center back edge, with right sides together and ¼ inch (.5 cm) seam allowance. Press seam allowances toward the facing.

4. Turn in the raw edge of each facing ½ inch (1 cm), then ½ inch (1 cm) again. Blindstitch to yoke.

5. Place yoke backs side by side and tack them together at the seamline.

6. Gather a strip of lace edging one and one-half times the total width of the back yoke lower edge. With right sides together, align the inner edge of the lace heading with the seamline. Stitch.

Sleeves

1. Cut sleeves from fabric.

2. Cut lace strips, using the width of the sleeve pattern as a guide. Assemble the strips as for the yoke.

3. Attach the trim to the lower edge of each sleeve.

4. Loosen upper thread tension slightly, and lengthen stitch slightly. On the right side of each sleeve, stitch around the cap along the seamline.

5. Adjust the machine settings and stitch the underarm seams.

CONSTRUCTING THE GOWN

1. Stitch yoke front to backs at shoulders using French seams.

2. Bind the neck edge with a bias strip of fabric (see page 40), finishing at the center back edges.

3. Cut skirt lengths from fabric. Use the lower section of the pattern to mark armholes.

4. If lace will be used around the lower edge, stitch it to each skirt section before sewing side seams. Stitch and clean finish the side seams.

5. For the sleeveless gown, bind the skirt portion of each armhole (see page 40).

6. Gather the upper edge of each skirt section, adjusting machine settings as for the sleeve. Pull the bobbin threads and gather the skirt

to fit the yoke. Stitch, with right sides together. Trim and overcast the seam allowances.

7. Pin the sleeves in place, pulling the bobbin threads and gathering the cap to fit. Stitch. Stitch again, 1/8 (3 mm) inch from the previous stitching line in the seam allowance. Trim close to stitching and overcast.

8. For the sleeveless gown, gather and stitch lace edging around the yoke portion of each armhole.

9. Hem the gown, or apply lace edging.

10. Sew a button and make a button loop at the back of the neck binding.

6. Heirloom Gifts

For a quick present or one that is months in the planning, a gift of
heirloom sewing expresses your thoughtfulness in a very special way.
On the following pages are suggestions to suit every gift-giving
occasion, each one certain to be appreciated for years to come.

Guest Towels

Even in our world of paper towels, dainty linen towels make a beautiful accessory for a powder room. They are so quick to make up that they can be ready to give to the hostess who called at the last minute with a dinner invitation. If time permits, add an embroidered motif or monogram for a personal touch.

Linen, as durable as it is beautiful, is the best fabric to use for these towels. Use a purchased linen towel for even quicker results.

MATERIALS
- Fabric, 21 by 14 inches (53 by 35 cm)
- Lace edging, or a combination entredeux, beading, and edging, 14 inch (35 cm) strips

CONSTRUCTION
1. Join lace strips, if more than one will be used, according to the heirloom sewing techniques described in Chapter 2.

2. Join the lace trim to one end of the towel.

3. Hem the remaining edges with narrow double hems.

4. Trim the lace extensions to $\frac{1}{2}$ inch (1 cm). To hem the ends, roll to the wrong side and whipstitch by hand.

Photo Album or Guest Book Cover

Especially thoughtful as a house-warming gift, the custom-covered guest book might be embroidered with the new address. And a photo album is always appreciated, doubly so when it is dressed up this way.

The cover can be decorated with even small scraps of eyelet or lace, and can be made of almost any fabric. With a very thin cover fabric, cut lining to the cover dimensions and stitch the pieces together around the outer edges as the first construction step.

MATERIALS

➤ Purchased album or guest book
➤ Fabric, according to measurements
➤ Assorted trims
➤ Beading, the length of the cover fabric
➤ Ribbon, the length of the beading plus ½ yard (.5 m)

MEASURING AND CUTTING

1. Measure the spine of the book from top to bottom and add 1 inch (2.5 cm). Use this measurement for fabric length.

2. For width, measure the book from the cover front edge, around the spine, to the cover back edge. Add 5 inches (13 cm). Cut fabric this width.

CONSTRUCTION

1. Fold fabric in half lengthwise to mark position for the beading along the spine. Stitch the beading in place and baste across the upper and lower edges.

2. Serge or overcast all fabric edges.

3. Stitch other trims onto the cover according to your design.

4. Fold each end 2½ inches (6.5 cm) to the right side. Stitch across the upper and lower edges with ⅜ inch (1 cm) seam allowance. Turn right side out. Fold under the seam allowance across the remainder of the top and bottom, and topstitch or blind hem.

5. Slip the book covers into the end pockets.

6. Thread ¼-inch (.7-cm) ribbon through the beading, open the book to the center and tie the ends of the ribbon snugly to anchor the cover.

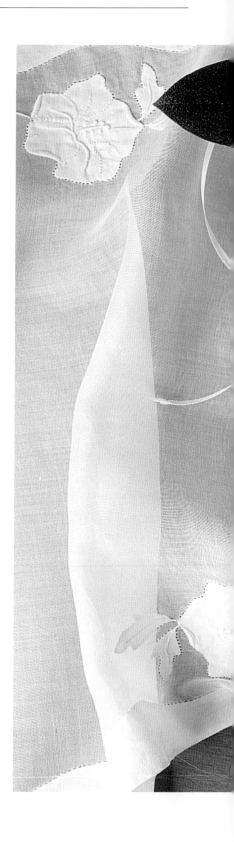

Hanger Cover

No one ever has enough good hangers. This cover offers enjoyment for its creator as well as practical service for the recipient. A padded inner cover helps keep the garment wrinkle free.

The design potential is unlimited—it can be made of beautiful fabric with just a touch of lace or trim added, or it could be made up entirely of laces, front and back. The cover shown is linen, with an ornate galloon strip across the center and narrow edging around the open lower edge.

MATERIALS
➤ Clothes hanger, preferably wood or heavy plastic
➤ Laces and trims, according to your design
➤ Fabric for outer cover, ⅜ yard (.35 m)
➤ Fabric for inner cover, ⅜ yard (.35 m)
➤ Polyester batting, ⅜ yard (.35 m)
➤ Ribbon, ½ yard (.5), for tie
➤ Lining fabric for the outer cover, if needed

CONSTRUCTION
1. Make a pattern for the inner cover. On a sheet of paper, trace around the outer edge of the hanger. Add seam allowance. Cut the pattern. Cut two of inner cover and batting.

2. Baste batting to the wrong side of the inner cover along the seamline. Trim away batting seam allowance.

3. With right sides together, stitch the lower edge and one shoulder. Turn and press. Slip the hanger into place. Whip remaining shoulder seam closed.

4. Outline the padded hanger on paper to make the outer cover pattern. Extend lines straight downward approximately 3 inches (7.5 cm) at the sides, then straight across for the lower edge. Add seam allowance and cut out the pattern. Cut two from fabric.

5. Assemble laces and trims to decorate the cover. You may choose to adorn only the front side of the cover, in which case lace ends can be sewn into the shoulder seams. For instructions on sewing laces, see Chapter 6.

6. Stitch the shoulder seams with right sides together, leaving an opening at the top to insert the hanger, and leaving open across the lower edge.

7. Complete the embellishment.

8. Slip cover over the hanger and secure with a bow around the hanger neck.

Apron

The gift of an apron to a hostess was at one time a common practice, but now happens so infrequently that many of us must resort to using dish towels to protect our clothing against cooking calamities. Perhaps it's time to reinstate a practical tradition in an especially beautiful manner.

Rows of tucks on the bib and skirt are sewn on separate strips of fabric, then sewn with the embroidered trims to the main fabric. The shoulder straps form carriers at the back for the waistline ties.

MATERIALS

➤ Fabric, 1½ yards (1.4 m), 45 inches (115 cm) wide
➤ Eyelet beading/entredeux, 1½ yards (1.4 m)
➤ Eyelet insertion/entredeux, 1½ yards (1.4 m)
➤ Eyelet edging, 1½ inches (4 cm) wide, ¼ yard (.25 m)
➤ Eyelet edging, 5¼ inches (13.5 cm) wide, 1¼ yards (1.15 m)

CONSTRUCTION

Detailed instructions for the heirloom sewing techniques are found in Chapter 2, beginning on page 20.

Cut fabric as shown in the diagram. Use ½ inch (1.3 cm) seam allowance for fabric seams; stitch lace seams according to the instruction.

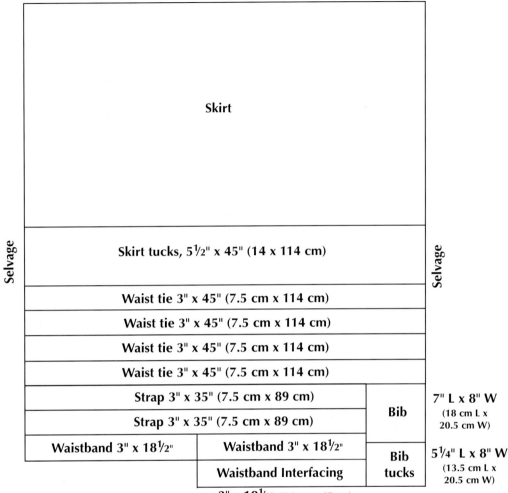

Apron cutting guide, 45 inch (114-115 cm) fabric.

Tuck strips

1. Mark the tuck foldlines on the bib tuck strip fabric section. Starting 1⅛ inches (2.8 cm) above the lower edge, snip into the 8-inch (20 cm) side at 1-inch (2.5 cm) intervals four times. Repeat on the opposite edge. Pull a thread between each pair of snips to mark the tuck foldlines.

2. Crease on the marked lines and stitch ¼ inch (.5 cm) from each crease. Press all tucks the same direction.

3. Mark and stitch the skirt tuck strip in the same way

In a soft cotton lawn print, the same apron has a more casual air. Try it with holiday fabrics, too!

Bib

1. Cut 8-inch (20-cm) strips of beading and insertion.

2. Working from the upper edge, join the eyelet strips. Stitch narrow eyelet edging to insertion with right sides together, stitching as closely as possible to the entredeux holes. Overcast with a close, narrow zigzag stitch; trim. Press flat.

3. Attach tuck strip in the same manner.

4. Attach the beading.

5. Sew lace panel to the fabric bib section.

Straps

1. With right side of strap to wrong side of bib, pin strap to each side of bib, aligning strap end with lower bib edge. Stitch. Press seam allowances toward strap.

2. Fold remaining long edge of strap ½ inch (1.3 cm) to wrong side; press.

3. Fold pressed edge of strap to just cover the previous stitching line on the bib right side; press. Pin in place.

4. Press under the raw edges of the strap extension, folding the end to the inside. Stitch close to the edge and across the end. Repeat for the other strap.

5. Form the waistline tie carriers. Fold the tie ends 1½ inches (4 cm) toward the wrong side of the bib. Pin, and try on the apron to check that the loops are at the waistline. Adjust if necessary. Stitch.

Skirt

1. Join trims for the skirt as for the bib. Beginning at the lower edge, stitch the wide edging to the insertion. Attach the tucked strip, then the beading.

2. Stitch the beading to the lower edge of the skirt.

3. Hem the sides. Turn each side 1½ inches (3 cm) to the wrong side; press. Turn in ½ inch (1 cm); press, and stitch.

Waistband and ties

1. Baste interfacing to the wrong side of one (the outer) waistband strip.

2. Center bib along interfaced band with right sides together and raw edges aligned. Baste.

3. Pin the remaining band section to the bib, band right side to bib wrong side, bib and band edges aligned. Stitch, continuing stitching to band ends. On the band facing long edge, press the seam allowance to the wrong side.

4. Turn band ends ½ inch (1.5 cm) to wrong side; press.

5. Pin two tie sections with right sides together. Stitch long the edges and across one end, angling the stitching line on the end to form a point. Turn right side out and press.

6. Gather the unfinished tie ends to fit the waistband. Baste to the folded seam allowance on the outer band section, aligning raw edges.

7. Gather upper edge of skirt to fit band. Pin and stitch to outer band section with right sides together. Press seam allowances toward band.

8. Fold band facing along seamline so pressed edge just covers the skirt stitching line. Topstitch bands together along the ends and skirt edge, stitching close to the edge of the band.

Lacy Lamb Pillow

He is cuddly enough to become a baby's favorite toy and elegant enough for a teenager's bedroom. He is guaranteed to be handed down as an heirloom!

Assemble a lace block for just the front and use an interesting fabric for the back, or make both sides of lace. For a striking effect, add a lining in a contrasting color.

MATERIALS

➤ Laces, a combination of beading, insertion, and entredeux, according to your design
➤ Ribbon, for beading and a neck bow
➤ Buttons for the eyes and nose
➤ Loose fiberfill for stuffing

CONSTRUCTION

Detailed instructions for the heirloom sewing techniques are found in Chapter 2, beginning on page 20.

1. Enlarge and cut out the pattern. Draw a rectangle slightly larger than the greatest length and width of the pattern and use the block as a guide for determining quantities and assembling the laces.

2. Join the lace strips for one or both sides.

3. Lay the pattern piece over the block and trace around the edges.

Stitch along the marked line and cut approximately ½ inch (1 cm) outside the line.

4. Stitch the pieces with right sides together, leaving an opening at the lower edge for turning. Turn right side out.

5. Fill with stuffing—not too firmly. Stitch across the opening.

6. Sew buttons at the marked positions. A word of caution: if this is to be a toy for a very young child, embroider the features instead of using buttons.

7. Sew the ear at the marked location.

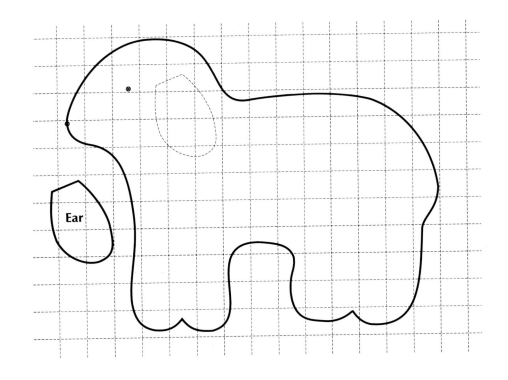

Ear

7. Special-Occasion Heirlooms

Certain milestones in the lives of good friends and loved ones deserve special commemoration. Those of us who sew are fortunate—we can call upon our abilities to produce a gift that will truly become a cherished heirloom. Such an event provides the perfect occasion to use treasured pieces and our most creative design ideas.

A Garter for the Bride

The traditional garter, lacy and white, is a gift that the bride will always appreciate when it comes from a friend. It can be embellished with any pretty lace (perhaps a scrap from the bride's gown) and beading threaded with blue ribbon.

Soft, lightweight fabric is best; silk or cotton batiste is especially elegant.

MATERIALS
➤ Elastic, non-roll, 1 inch (2.5 cm) wide, cut to leg measurement plus 1 inch (2 cm)
➤ Fabric, in length, two and one-half times length of elastic; 6 inches (15 cm) wide
➤ Lace edging, the length of fabric, or combination of laces

CONSTRUCTION
1. Cut fabric on the fabric cross-grain.

2. Join laces, if necessary, according to the heirloom techniques described in Chapter 2, page 20.

3. Clean finish one long edge of fabric and attach lace edging.

4. Clean finish remaining long edge of fabric, turn under ½ inch (1 cm), and press. Unfold the pressed edge and sew ends of strip with

right sides together to form a circle. Press. Re-fold the pressed edge.

5. Join ends of elastic, overlapping by ½ inch (1 cm). Stitch securely.

6. Hold the fabric circle wrong side out and slip the elastic circle over it, matching seams. Fold the pressed fabric edge around the elastic. Stitch close to the elastic but not through it.

Ring Bearer's Pillow

Although it appears very complicated, the design is quite simple. This is an occasion for going all-out, using the most beautiful French ribbon you can find. As an alternative, make up your own "ribbon" from a combination of insertion laces. The only requirement is that the ribbon at the center, to be tied around the wedding ring, should be sewn *very* securely. The cover can be removed for cleaning, ready to be used by a daughter or granddaughter some day.

MATERIALS
➤ Pillow form, 12 inches (30.5 cm) square
➤ Fabric for front, back, and ruffle (see step 1)
➤ Lace edging, 2½ yards (2.3 m) French ribbon, 1¼ yards (1.15 m), 2½ inches (6.5 cm) wide
➤ Narrow ribbon, ½ yard (.5 m), for ring tie
➤ Button

INSTRUCTIONS
Detailed instructions for the heirloom sewing techniques needed for assembling the cover front are found in Chapter 2, beginning on page 20.

1. From fabric, cut pillow front section 13 by 13 inches (33 by 33 cm), or size of pillow form plus seam allowances. Cut two pillow back sections 13 by 10 inches (33 by 25 cm). Cut two strips for the ruffle, 4 by 48 inches (10 by 122 cm).

2. Hem one long edge of each pillow back section with a 1-inch (2.5 cm) double hem. Make a buttonhole at the center of one hem.

3. Overlap the hems so the back is the size of the front. Baste backs together across the ends in the seam allowances. Sew a button on the underlying hemmed edge.

4. Arrange French ribbon to form a square on the pillow front. Miter the corners. Stitch in place along both edges.

5. Sew the center of the ribbon to the center of the pillow top, stitching it securely.

6. To make the ruffle, join the ends of the fabric strips with French seams to form a circle. Clean finish one long edge. Join the ends of the lace edging to form a circle. Sew the lace to the finished fabric edge.

7. Sew gathering stitch along the unfinished fabric edge and mark it into quarters. Gather the ruffle to the pillow top with right sides together.

8. Stitch the cover back to the front with right sides together, keeping ruffle and ribbon ends free. Trim and overcast the seam.

Christening Gown

A special dress for baby's christening may be the archetypal heirloom garment, many of them worn and cherished by several generations. This distinctive design was inspired by a doll dress that was given to the author when she was 8 years old.

Fine Swiss cotton batiste is the traditional fabric for a christening gown and cap. It is a good choice for the slip, too. The dress is sized for a newborn baby.

MATERIALS

For dress and slip
- Fabric, 2 yards (1.85 m)
- Lace beading, 1¾ yards (1.6 m)
- Ribbon, ¼ inch (.7 cm) wide, for the beading, 1¾ yards (1.6 m)
- Ribbon, ⅛ inch (3 mm) wide, for the sleeves, ¾ yard (.7 m)
- Narrow lace insertion, 3 yards (2.75 m)
- Narrow lace edging, 2½ yards (2.4 m)
- Wide lace edging, 2¼ yards (2.2 m)
- 3 to 8 very small pearl buttons for the dress back, or 3 beauty pins
- Elastic, 1/16 inch (2 mm) wide, ½ yard (.5 m)
- Small clear snaps

CUTTING

1. Enlarge and cut out the pattern pieces (page 126).

2. Cut the pattern pieces from fabric, using the layout as a guide. Use the gown back and back yoke pattern pieces for the slip back and back yoke.

3. Cut bias strips 1½ inches wide for the dress and slip necklines, and for the slip armholes.

CONSTRUCTION

For a neatly finished gown, use French seams. Instructions are on page 40.

Detailed instructions for the heirloom sewing techniques are found in Chapter 2, beginning on page 20.

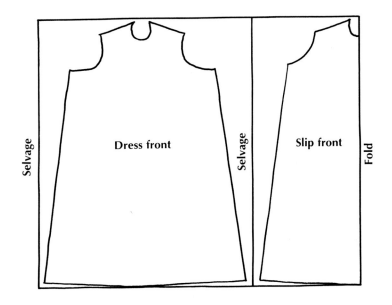

Cutting layout for christening dress and slip, 45 inch (114–115 cm) fabric.

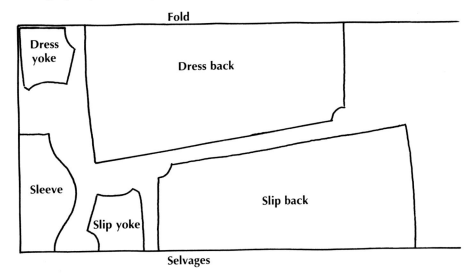

Gown Front

1. Tape dress front over the pattern piece and lightly trace the lace placement lines.

2. Baste along the marked gathering line at each armhole. Do not gather or cut yet.

3. Cut strips of lace insertion for the front Vs, allowing enough length to overlap by 1 inch (2.5 cm) at the points and extend slightly into the beading placement area.

4. Place each pair of lace strips with right sides together and stitch at a 45 degree angle to form the points. Trim and overcast the seam allowances.

5. Position the Vs, right side up, within the placement lines on the gown front.

6. Straight stitch the lace in place, stitching along the inner edge of both headings. Break stitching along the lower edge of the upper V at the beading placement point so that the upper end of the beading strip can be tucked under the lace.

7. Pin lace strips over the gathering line at each upper side, with the end extending 1/4 inch (.5 cm) into the beading placement area. Stitch only along the upper heading of the strip.

8. Lift the lace and cut just below the seamline and above the gathering stitches to the beading line.

9. Gather the side extension to fit the lace, and pin to the lace lower edge. Stitch along the lace heading. From the wrong side, trim the gathered edge close to the stitching.

10. Cut beading, planning so that the holes will be aligned across the front panel.

11. Pin the beading along the placement lines. Tuck the upper ends under the lace V and overlap the inner ends of the side strips. Straight stitch along both sides of both strips of beading.

12. Thread ribbon through the beading. Starting at the top, bring ribbon out at the first hole so that threading will be the same for both beading strips. Tuck the upper ribbon ends under the lace V.

13. Stitch over all the previous lace stitching lines with a zigzag stitch. Use a stitch width barely wider than the lace heading.

14. *Very carefully* trim away fabric behind the lace Vs, trimming close to the zigzag stitching. Trim the lace ends behind the beading. If desired, trim fabric from behind beading too.

Gown back and neckline

1. Gather upper edge of each skirt back to fit yoke. Pin, with right sides together, and stitch.

2. Turn in facings along back sections 3/8 inch (1 cm), then 3/8 inch (1 cm) again; blindstitch.

3. Sew the backs to front at shoulders.

4. Cut a strip of lace 12 inches (30 cm) long and gather it to fit the neck edge. Hem each end by rolling the raw edge toward the wrong side and securing with stitches. Pin and baste the lace along the neck seamline, right side up on the gown right side.

5. Bind the neckline with a bias fabric strip as described on page 40.

Sleeves and side seams

1. Baste around upper edge for gathering.

2. Sew lace edging to lower edge. With right sides together, position lace 1/8 inch (3 mm) inside sleeve edge, and straight stitch along inner border of lace. Press seam toward sleeve. From the right side, topstitch close to the seamline to keep seam allowance in place. Trim seam allowances close to stitching.

3. Cut elastic the same length as sleeve lower edge. Position it over the guide line and zigzag over it, encasing the elastic but not catching it in the stitching.

4. Draw up elastic to a length of approximately 7 inches (18 cm). Tack securely at each end and trim the excess.

5. Gather upper edge of sleeve to fit armhole and stitch with right sides together.

6. Pin back to front at sides, and pin sleeve underarm seam. Stitch in a continuous seam.

7. Tie ⅛ inch (3 mm) ribbon loosely over the elastic around each sleeve. Tack in place at the underarm seamline.

Hem and finishing

1. Cut lace insertion the measurement of the gown lower edge plus 1 inch (2 cm). Cut edging one and one-half times this length and gather to fit the insertion. Pin the insertion to the edging, with the border of the insertion overlapping the border of the edging. Stitch with a straight stitch, then with a zigzag stitch.

2. Pin the insertion to the gown lower edge with right sides together, the lace ¼ inch (.5 cm) from the gown edge, leaving ½ inch (1 cm) free at each end of the lace.

Straight stitch along the lace border. Press seam toward gown.

3. Hem the ends of the lace by rolling them to the wrong side and stitching by hand.

4. On the outside, topstitch close to the seamline to keep seam allowance in place.

5. If buttons will be used, work buttonholes along the back yoke edge.

Slip

1. Cut the front from the slip pattern. Use the dress back and back yoke pieces for the slip back.

2. Finish center back yoke edges as for the dress back.

3. Sew shoulder seams.

4. Gather the upper edge of the back skirt section and stitch to the yokes.

5. Stitch the side seams.

6. Bind the armholes and neckline as described on page 40.

7. Apply lace to the lower edge as for the dress.

8. Sew buttons or snaps along the center back opening.

Christening Cap

MATERIALS

➤ Fabric to match gown, 7 by 13½ inches (18 by 34 cm)
➤ Lace edging for rosettes, ¾ yard (.7 m), cut in half
➤ Narrow lace edging for cap front, ⅜ yard (.35 m)
➤ Narrow lace insertion for cap, ⅜ yard (.35 m)
➤ Double-faced satin ribbon, ¼ inch (.7 cm) wide, 1 yard (.95 m)

CONSTRUCTION

1. For the cap front, join the lace edging to the insertion.

2. Attach the insertion to one long edge of the fabric strip, the right side of the lace against the wrong side of the fabric. Clean finish seam allowances and press toward fabric.

3. Fold the fabric, right side out, ½ inch (1.5 cm) from the lace seam to create a fabric border along the front edge of the cap.

4. Hem each end with a ¼-inch (.5-cm) double hem.

5. Form a casing at the back. Turn the back edge ⅝ inch (1.5 cm) to the wrong side; press. Turn the raw edge under ¼ inch (.5 cm); press and stitch close to the fold.

6. Thread a 12-inch (30-cm) length of ribbon through the casing. Draw up the edge tightly and tie a bow.

7. Make rosettes. Pull a thread in the lace heading and gather the lace tightly so that it forms a circle. Whip the ends together.

8. Tack a bow at the center of each rosette. Stitch a rosette near the lower edge of the cap on each side.

Christmas Stocking

Copy the pattern in the size it's shown to make up tiny stockings to hang on the tree or as elegant "wrapping" for the smallest gift. Enlarge it by photocopier to standard stocking size; or make it larger still for a holiday-season pillow or wall hanging.

Bits of laces and trims saved from other projects can be put to good use in trimming the stocking tops.

As for fabric, scraps of velvet and bright holiday plaids will be just right. Or just for fun, experiment with combinations of eyelets or laces in an overall design. Finished with the narrowest of ribbons, it's a perfect gift for baby's first Christmas.

MATERIALS
- Fabric, for the stocking
- Lining fabric
- Facing fabric: stocking fabric or a complementary material
- Assorted trims, laces, and ribbons

CONSTRUCTION

Detailed instructions for the steps that involve heirloom sewing techniques are found in Chapter 2, beginning on page 20. Use ⅝ inch (1.5 cm) seam allowance except where instructed otherwise.

1. Enlarge the pattern to the desired size and cut it out.

2. Cut two stocking and two lining pieces. Cut two facing sections from upper part of pattern, either of stocking fabric or contrasting

fabric according to instructions for the design you will use.

3. For a hanger, stitch a fabric tube approximately ¾ inch (2 cm) wide and 5 inches (13 cm) long, or shorter for a small stocking. As an alternative, use a length of ribbon.

4. Sew the stocking sections with right sides together. Trim, clip seam allowance around the curves, and turn. Press.

5. Sew lining in the same way, but do not turn. Slip lining into stocking, wrong sides together, and baste the upper edges together.

6. With right sides together, join ends of facing to form a circle. Press.

7. Slip facing into stocking, right sides together. Double the hanger piece and incorporate into the seam at center back between stocking and facing, ends aligned with stocking and facing edges. Stitch facing to stocking and lining.

Clean finish seam allowances and press toward facing.

8. Make and attach the cuff according to your design plan. Cut cuff trims to the circumference of the finished stocking facing edge, adding seam allowance at the ends. Cut ribbons about three times that length to allow for a bow.

Design 1, left
Fabric and facing: blue cotton velveteen
Trims: wide embroidered edging, plaid ribbon

CONSTRUCTION

1. Attach edging to the outer facing edge.

2. Pin ribbon over edging seamline, starting with the center of the ribbon at center back. On the right side, stitch along both edges of the ribbon, leaving the ends free at the front to tie.

Design 2, second left
Fabric and facing: Plaid cotton
Trims: Wide eyelet edging, ribbon

CONSTRUCTION

1. Join insertion to beading, then join this piece to the white cotton.

2. Sew the cotton to the facing edge, right sides together. Thread ribbon through the beading.

Design 3, second right
Fabric: Black cotton velveteen
Facing: White cotton
Trims: Embroidered beading with entredeux, embroidered edging, ribbon for beading

CONSTRUCTION

1. Attach edging to beading/entredeux.

2. Attach beading/entredeux to facing. Thread ribbon through beading.

Design 4, right
Fabric and facing: Light blue cotton velveteen
Trim: Lace edging, embroidered ribbon

CONSTRUCTION

1. Cut lace one and one-half times the upper stocking circumference. Gather lace and stitch to outer facing edge.

2. Pin ribbon over lace seamline, starting with the center of the ribbon at center back. On the right side, stitch along both edges of ribbon to center front, leaving the ribbon ends free to tie.

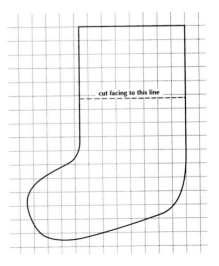

cut facing to this line

1 square = 1 inch (2.5 cm)

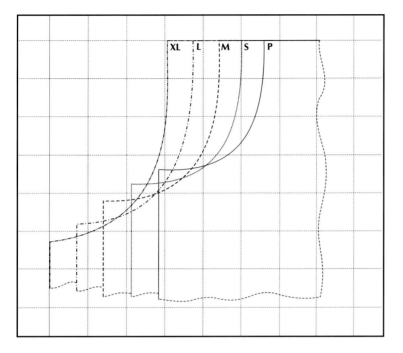

Cutting guide for lower armhole,
Quick Camisole, page 53, and
Summer Nightgown, page 87.

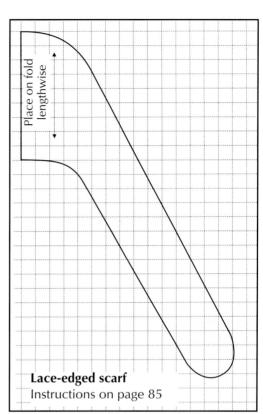

Lace-edged scarf
Instructions on page 85

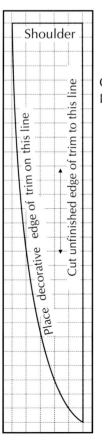

Shoulder

Place decorative edge of trim on this line

Cut unfinished edge of trim to this line

Place on fold lengthwise

Cutting guide for ruffle
Instructions on page 81

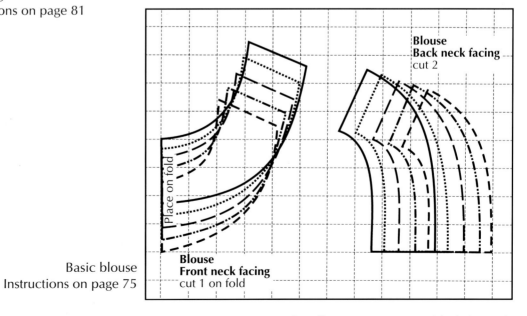

**Blouse
Back neck facing**
cut 2

Place on fold

**Blouse
Front neck facing**
cut 1 on fold

Basic blouse
Instructions on page 75

For all patterns 1 square = 1 inch (2.5 cm)

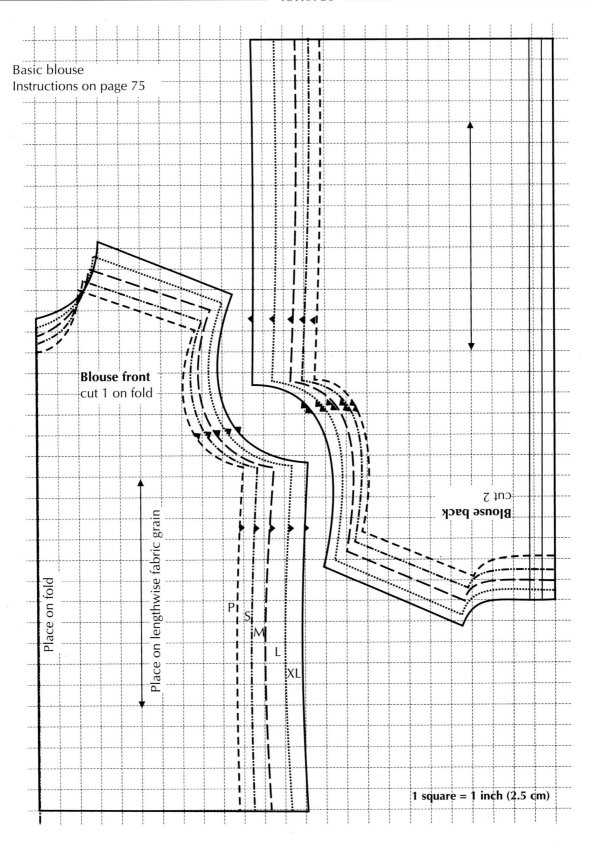

Basic blouse
Instructions on page 75

Blouse front
cut 1 on fold

Place on fold

Place on lengthwise fabric grain

P
S
M
L
XL

Blouse back
cut 2

1 square = 1 inch (2.5 cm)

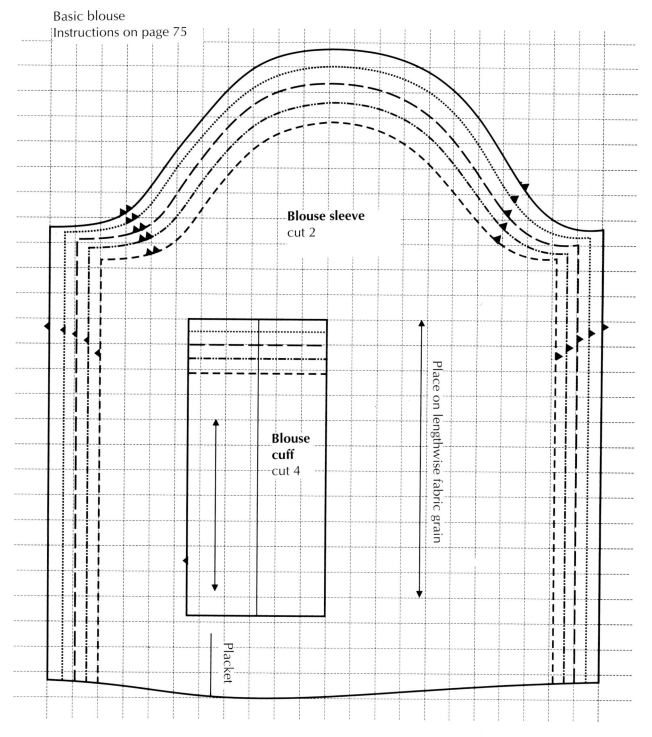

Basic blouse
Instructions on page 75

Blouse sleeve
cut 2

Blouse cuff
cut 4

Place on lengthwise fabric grain

Placket

1 square = 1 inch (2.5 cm)

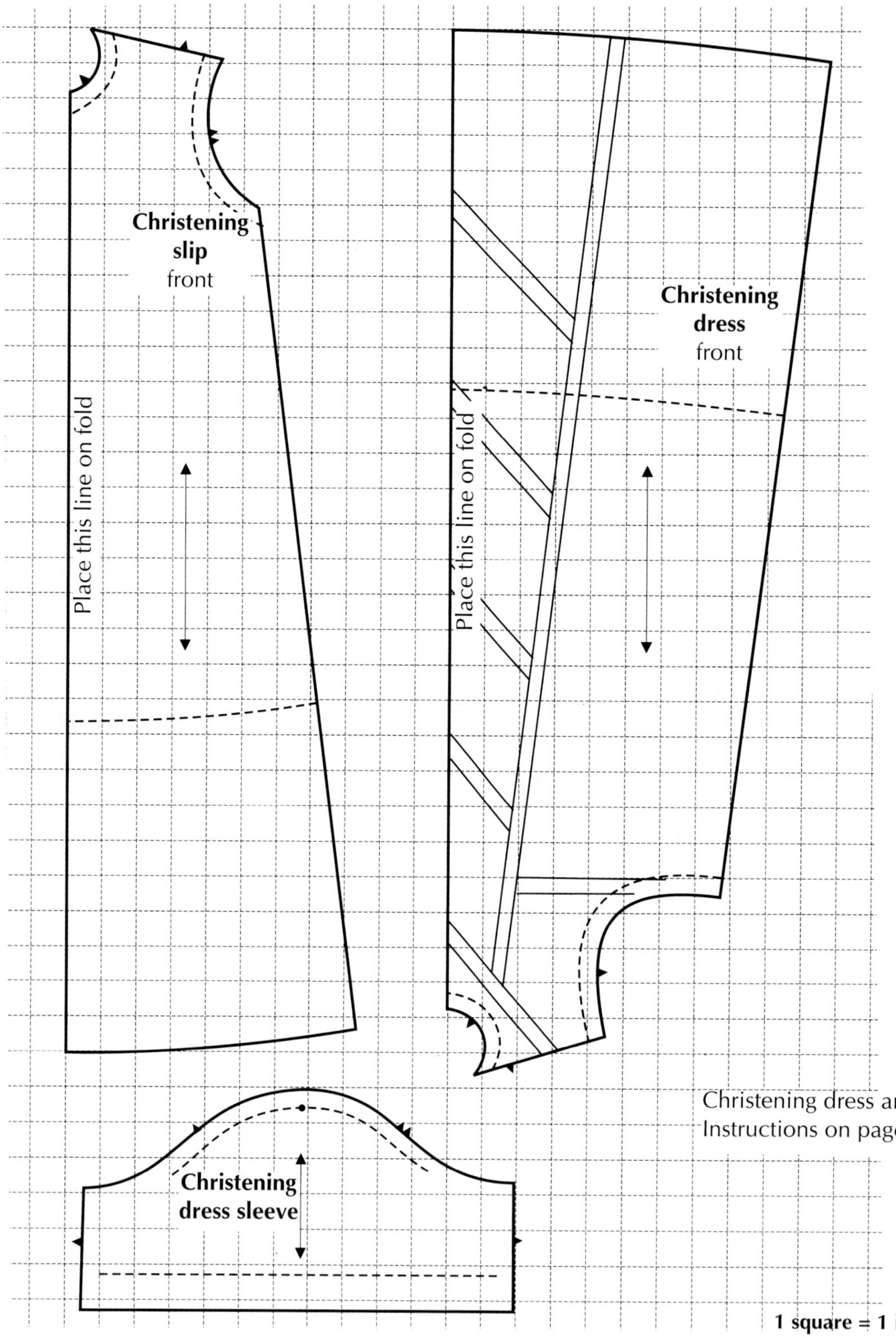

Christening slip
front

Place this line on fold

Christening dress
front

Place this line on fold

Christening dress sleeve

Christening dress and slip
Instructions on page 117–120

1 square = 1 inch (2.5 cm)

Christening dress and slip
Instructions on page 117–120

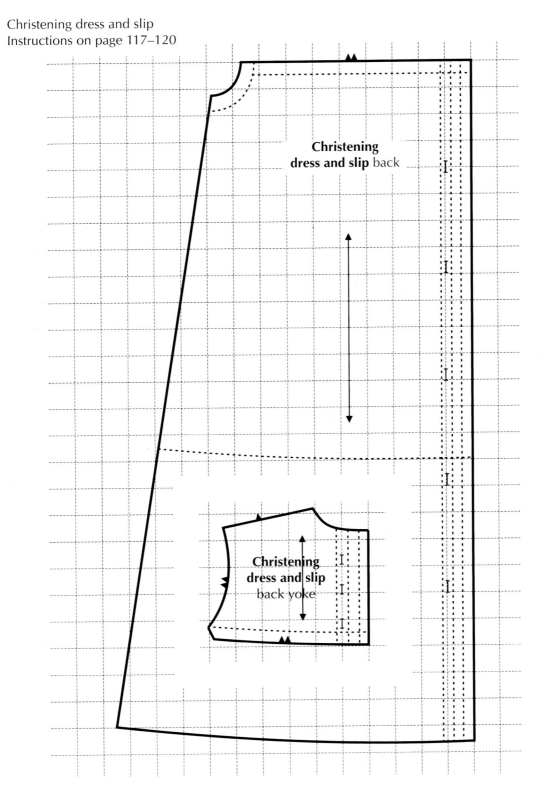

**Christening
dress and slip** back

**Christening
dress and slip
back yoke**

1 square = 1 inch (2.5 cm)

Index

Publisher's Acknowledgements

The staff at Lark Books wish to express our heartfelt thanks to the author for the hospitality she extended our crew during the photography for this book at her beautiful home, *Chestnut Logs*. We wish also to thank the owners of *Saluda Cottages*, in Flat Rock, North Carolina, for allowing us to photograph at their home.

Editor's Note

The reader may have wondered at the juxtaposition of a moth among the heirloom fabrics on the preceding pages. This beautiful moth, *Actias luna*, was discovered during the photography for the book and its grace and delicacy seemed a fine complement to manmade materials exhibiting those same qualities. The luna is *not* a fabric foe. The caterpillar eats leaves of sweet gum and other trees; the adult doesn't feed at all.